SO FAR . . .

SO GOOD . . . SO THERE!

Lowell Thomas

iUniverse, Inc.
Bloomington

SO FAR . . . SO GOOD . . . SO THERE!

iUniverse books may be ordered through booksellers or by contacting:

iUniverse
1663 Liberty Drive
Bloomington, IN 47403
www.iuniverse.com
1-800-Authors (1-800-288-4677)

ISBN: 978-1-4620-3611-0 (sc)
ISBN: 978-1-4620-3579-3 (ebk)

Printed in the United States of America

iUniverse rev. date: 08/17/2011

DEDICATION

When I sent the Prologue of this book to brother Bruce, long before it was complete, he responded with, "I think your next book should be titled, *So Far . . . So Good . . . So Long . . . So There!* Not wishing to write another book about my life, because at age 75 I figured there wouldn't be that much to write about. Instead, I decided upon a compromise. Besides, the words "So Long" in the title can have a rather negative image. I then came up with the current title for this Pulitzer Prize memoir.

So to Bruce, my youngest brother, whom I dearly love, and who has inspired me in ways he will never know, I spare my descendants (and others?) the boredom of never having to read Volume III . . . and to him I dedicate this book with gratitude. So there!

PROLOGUE

While waiting for Jane during her physical therapy sessions following her total knee replacement surgery on November 14, 2005, I would take along a copy of *So Far . . . So Good; The Other Lowell Thomas Story.* It was the first volume of my autobiography, and I was re-reading it to try to determine where I should take off on *So Far . . . So Good . . . So There!*

As we were leaving her physical therapy session that day and heading for the parking lot, I remarked to her, "Do you realize I have had a beard for thirty-three years?" I had made similar remarks about other events of my life in the book that had been buried in memory for a long time. Without skipping a beat, she replied, limping to the car, "You are learning a lot about yourself, aren't you?"

I guess I was, as some of the things I read in the first volume of my autobiography were as new to me as to someone who had never known me. I suspect that is somewhat common for an aging memory, or else it's because, as someone once said, "It's because there is so much up there (in the memory part of the brain) due to the age of the person, the old stuff is being pushed out by the new stuff." I prefer to think it is the latter.

Someone also has mentioned that age is merely in the mind, and that you are as young as you feel. While I somewhat believe that, I was having a tough time convincing myself as, over the years, I had had prostate surgery, umbilical hernia surgery and numerous aches and pains and surgeries related to arthritis.

Nevertheless, time marches on and as I reviewed my history I was rewarded by the e-mails I had received from friends and oh, yes, a dear relative, my brother Bruce. Those I didn't hear from I merely wrote them off as saying "OK, another passage from another scribe." But from those I heard from about *So Far . . . So Long; the Other Lowell Thomas Story,* I cherished their comments and include some of them here:

From old friends, Rex and Sharon Conely: *We read your book, Lowell. Interesting and so well written—We marvel at being able to write so smoothly. We sat down to just look at it, and much later was still reading. What a legacy for your children and their children. Wouldn't it be great if more people did that! We'd understand the generations better.*

Rex and I had been best of friends at Western Michigan University in the late 1950s when we both "reveled" in the U.S. Army Reserves in Kalamazoo.

Then came a message from sweet Laura. Laura was Brenda's best friend from junior high school through high school and was the former's maid of honor at her wedding in 1982.

Laura is a Scandinavian blonde, a model in stature and someone in whom all of us would someday confide. She grew up in a home with a step-mother who seldom appreciated Laura's virtues even though the step-mother was a fine and generous person herself. Sometimes Laura would accompany us on family vacations enjoyed in our old camper with the Sunfish sailboat strapped securely on the top.

Laura eventually married a college-turned-professional-turned-college football coach and produced an equally wonderful son and a pair of twins; a boy and girl. As of this writing (2009), Frank is the head football coach for Boston College, having gone there from coaching in a professional league in Calgary.

Laura wrote: *Lowell, your book was very interesting and heartwarming. What always came through was how you and Jane just really are best of friends and were always there for each other. Being married, one appreciates that so much more! I enjoyed the travel portions very much, but I particularly enjoyed reading about your family life as I remember a lot of what you wrote. I was excited to see my name in print! Unfortunately, I so vaguely remember doing anything so corrupt. Thanks for reminding me—I had a good chuckle!!*

Then there was Bruce, my younger brother by nine years. Part of his story is also told in the first volume of this history. We were close, I suppose partly, because he lived with Jane and me during his final year in high school, as mentioned in the former book. Bruce, receiving his copy of the first volume in December 2000, wrote:

Well Bro, I finished your book and wanted to give you some feedback, although you haven't asked for it. Ya know what they say about free advice, hmmm, what is THAT they say??

I liked it. So there. It is quite a document of your personal history.

I really liked how you presented it, e.g., the cover, the title, your hand-writing on the front, pictures of your face(s). May I be the first (?) to note that since your were a young sailor (actually, I was a soldier), *you are parting your hair on the "other" side. Nice touch.* (I don't know what that had to do with anything, but that's Bruce).

Of course, being the brother of the author, I was interested in what the hell you have been doing with your life since I moved out! I was somewhat amazed at all the traveling you have been doing. Although you have told me through the years that you have gone hither and yon, but having it all down on paper and reading it in a short period of time put it in a different perspective.

I must also say that you brought me to tears on more than one occasion. Thanks a lot! Seriously, that is not a bad thing and my tears were not always of the sad variety.

I also liked your one-liners that you quoted to introduce each chapter. Very fitting. (I thought they were too, but Bruce was the only one who ever mentioned it). *I was disappointed, however, that you never quoted me in some of my classic sayings, like, "Huh?" But I have gotten passed that.*

I could go on, but don't want your ego to get too inflated. I do have the title for your NEXT book. Keep in mind that someone else will have to put the finishing touches on it. (I'm not certain what Bruce had in mind here). *"So Far . . . So Good . . . So Long . . . So There!" Hey, just a thought, and like I started to say about free advice above . . . .*

But undoubtedly the most profound and appreciated remarks came from a 14-year-old, who is a college senior as this is being written (2008). Grandson, Kevin, e-mailed me on April 18, 2001:

I forgot to tell you in the last letter I wrote that I am in the middle of reading your book! I LOVE IT! Once I started reading it I just can't put it down! I am already on Chapter 14. I really like reading about all the things in your life, Grandpa, and it is very interesting to me! I read it at school and a few times my teachers have been curious and have asked, "What are you reading?" Without skipping a beat I reply, "My grandfather's autobiography!" I am very proud of it and I am very proud to say, "My Grandpa wrote this book!" I have showed all of my friends it and even some who aren't my friends. I just wanted to let you know that I am very proud of you and I believe that you are a GREAT author!!!

Love ya lots -Kevin

Wow! That blew my mind. But Kevin has surprised Jane and me more than once with his literary talents. On occasion he has been known to bring a tear to our eyes due to his great way with words.

Oh, yes, and the former book took on an international flair in December of 2000. Through our travels we became familiar with two families in New Zealand; Vivian and Mike Spriggs and Pete and Anne Heffernan.

Upon reading the book, Anne e-mailed and said, in part, *It is a wonderful gift you have Lowell, and to put it in a book for others to enjoy is great!*

OK, enough ego injection, and now, as Paul Harvey, a once-famous newscaster would say, ". . . for the rest of the story."

CHAPTER ONE

To ignore the facts does not change the facts.

__Before__ **the rest of the story, however,** I must correct an error I wrote in the first Volume. If it weren't so important I would dismiss it as just a mistake, but it is important to the history of the family.

On page 9 of *So Far . . . So Good . . .* I wrote; *Besides two sisters and a brother, Mother had a noteworthy relative. Her uncle, my great-uncle had been in the Civil War. In a newspaper clipping I came across years later, I learned he had been wounded in the Battle of the Wilderness. Under the command of Ulysses S. Grant, 17,000 men lost their lives. After Great-Uncle returned home to heal, he headed west to fight with General George Custer. Fortunately Great-Uncle was not with Custer during his last stand.*

Great-Uncle was more than a fighter, however, as his obituary pointed out. When he died he left nine heirs; several of each gender.

WRONG! It was not my Great-Uncle at all. It was my Great-Grandfather! My mother's Grandfather.

I will be forever grateful to my Aunt Beulah and Uncle Oren of Lake Odessa (MI), having read Volume One, for correcting the error. He was also Uncle Oren's grandfather.

My problem was, however, that when I was writing Volume I, I was going by memory. Something I have long since learned never to trust. I knew Bruce had Mom's little scrapbook of memories and in it was Great-Granddad's obituary. I e-mailed Bruce and asked him to send pertinent details. For the sake of family history I include here, some of those details.

Orren (yup, two "r's") Daniels was born near Albany, NY on September 16, 1838. He died in Sebewa (MI) on April 17, 1921, of pneumonia at the age of 82.

During the Civil War, he enlisted in Company E., Sixth Michigan Cavalry on October 9, 1862.

Great-granddad Daniels was wounded in the Battle of the Wilderness on May 6, 1864. He was taken prisoner in the Battle of Appomattox and later returned to his ranks during an exchange of prisoners. He was then sent to the West to fight under General George Custer to assist in quelling the Indians.

He was honorably discharged at Fort Leavenworth, Kansas on November 24, 1865, with the rank of First Sergeant.

He married Sarah Kinney of Portland, MI who preceded him in death by twelve years.

In addition, Great-granddad was in the first graduating class of Michigan Agricultural College, which is now Michigan State University. The College was first established in 1855, making his graduation about 1859. I graduated from the same institution with my Specialist in Continuing Education (Ed.S.) Degree 113 years later and son David received his M.A. from MSU in 2004, making his graduation 145 years following his Great-great-Granddad's.

There! I have nobly corrected my error, and given Great-granddad Daniels his due.

After receiving those details, a friend in Plantation Estates Mobile Home Park in Ft. Myers showed me how to look up Great-Granddad on the Internet. I merely typed in the Company in which he fought and sure enough, there was Orren Daniels on the Company roster.

Having cleared that from my conscience, "the rest of the story," will include many of the travels Jane and I have enjoyed. As stated in the original volume, we decided that as long as our health and finances held out, we would do all the traveling we could during the decade of our 60s. Obviously both held, and as we hit 70 we were still traveling and/or planning traveling. So, also obviously, this discourse will include many of those travels. If nothing else, it helps me reinforce the fact that we have actually done all that traveling; sometimes by ourselves and often with our good friends, Dave and Jan Weissenborn and/or Curt and Peggy Young. Although Dave and Jan were both teachers in the Bullock Creek School District, in Midland, we really never became acquainted until Dave and I were both members of the Board of Directors of the Midland Teachers Credit Union (now Members First Credit Union). We became acquainted with Curt and Peggy from Matteson, IL when we first rented units side-by-side at Plantation Estates.

The first volume of *So Far . . . So Good . . .* ended in 2000 and the beginning of a new century. Much has happened since that time. Mostly good at the time of this writing.

CHAPTER TWO

Liking your wife is as important as loving her.

For over fifty years, Jane and I have sent to friends and family, a Christmas Letter. In all that time, we have missed only one year. That was the year David was born (December 7, 1963), and we were so busy with his health problems that we simply didn't have time or inclination to write. While Christmas Letters can be an irritation to many people, we have tried to write them in a light and often humorous manner. Only once, in all that time, did I receive a complaint. That was from Jane who thought it (I don't remember the year) a bit boastful; something we tried to avoid.

In fact, one year, prior to the Christmas season, I wrote a letter to nationally published advice-giver, Ann Landers, suggesting how to make family Christmas Letters less deplorable. Landers had, for years, bashed those who wrote them. I suspect she mentally bashed my "less deplorable" letter because my letter was never published. I guess I showed her!

I mention this referral to Christmas Letters only because *in* those were the most important happenings in our lives each year.

In addition, soon after completing the first Volume, I established a "Trigger File." In this I included things I wanted to be certain to include in this volume. Some items were copies of e-mails, either sent or received. All these items would "trigger" memories.

I might mention also, referring to the "ego injection," that during the time of publication of Volume One, it was fashionable for one to write one's memoirs. I put out my shingle and offered to teach people how to do it. I did this several times and sometimes was even paid for it. I labeled it, "From Memories to Memoirs." Shortly thereafter, I learned that "memoirs" are only certain memories, not necessarily one's life story. So I called it what it was, "Writing Your Autobiography." And later, I learned that some people actually did. The teacher in me just wouldn't go away!

I had meant to mention earlier, if I hadn't in Volume One, that in the early 1990s I had my own radio program over WGDN in Gladwin, owned by Steve Costin. It was called, "Thomas Tidbits for Today." It was only two to three minutes each day, but Steve pretty much gave me free reign over its contents.

On August 16, 1993, I broadcast the following:

"They had known each other since fourth grade, although they had never been sweethearts until many years later, following their graduation from high school, his military stint, and she, a senior in college.

"At 22 he realized she was the most beautiful, wonderful person he had ever known. They were married, and within the next five years produced the most delightful children the world would ever know.

"This wonderful, witty woman saw him through his college years by bringing home the pay check, thus meeting the bills.

"Whenever he disagreed with her she found a diplomatic way to work things out—and eventually it always worked out to the advantage of both.

"He placed her on a pedestal as she continued working hard to support their ideas, their dreams and their ambitions, and she enhanced his love for her through so many unselfish and often unsaid ways.

"She laughed with him and laughed at him, and she would laugh when she heard his corny jokes for the 20th time . . . and they became even closer.

"When times were tough, she was there to see him through them. When times were on a high, she was there to ride the wave with him.

"This lady could read him like a book, and more often than not, she served his every need before he knew he needed <u>anything</u>.

"When he was discouraged she saw to it that he could <u>begin</u> that word with an 'en.' When he was down, she let him know in her own inimitable, loving way, that he was, certainly, not out.

"When he hurt, she hurt. And sometimes, when her own aches and pains became nearly unbearable, she still put him first.

I know that beautiful, wonderful and witty woman well. You see, she became by bride . . . 35 years ago . . . today.

"Happy anniversary, sweetheart.

"That's Thomas Tidbits for today. I'm Lowell Thomas, saying . . . so long until tomorrow." (The last sentence is how my namesake, for fifty years, ended all his newscasts. I was a copy cat and many people of my generation remembered it).

CHAPTER THREE

A new millennium; Page One

I didn't often make first page of the *Midland Daily News*, but I did on January 1, 2000, the beginning of a new millennium. Ralph Wirtz, Managing Editor of the paper, knew we had visited New Zealand and asked me to renew any contacts and have them update me on any changes they saw regarding the new century and to write a story for the paper.

I did that and following is that front-page story:

New Zealanders say A-OK to Y2K . . . Hurray!

Fifty-five million sheep were among the first inhabitants on Earth to welcome in the new millennium.

They live, graze and raise families on the sleepy, sloping hillsides and pastures of New Zealand, and they could not care less about something called the "Y2K Bug."

But their owners do, as they are among the 3.8 million humans who live on the two major islands of New Zealand. It is the humans there who were some of the very first to celebrate the new millennium, and it is they who would have been first affected if preparations for the transition hadn't gone smoothly.

New Zealand started the year 2000 18 hours ahead of Washington, D.C., 13 hours ahead of the United Kingdom and five hours or so before its Asian neighbors, says Basil Logan, chairman of the Y2K Readiness Commission. Other countries watched closely to see if they could learn anything from what happened in New Zealand once the clock ticked past midnight on Dec. 31.

But smoothly it went.

At 11:07 on New Year's Eve, New Zealand resident and friend of the author of this article, Peter Heffernan said, "Our plan tonight went slightly overtime due to data backups taking longer than expected, but all in all we are happy with the results and it has proved that all our simulations of the event have been worthwhile.

"The city is just starting to come alive; mostly at a party in downtown Invercargill. The police are out in force and are being very visible."

By New Year's Day 2000 in New Zealand, long before Peter Jennings of New York had said, "All is well in New Zealand," Heffernan reported, "We made it. It's now about eight minutes into the new millennium here. Everyone still has lights and power, and our PC didn't even blink as the date changed smoothly to 2000."

"We are now into the year 2000," confirmed Lynne Krivan, another resident the author met when touring the South Seas a year ago. "It has been reported that the crowds all over the country have been very well behaved, just like normal New Year's Eve. All is well that ends well. Hope your country fares the same."

Heffernan began as a computer programmer in 1983, working for the Bank of New Zealand, but currently works for Southland Building Society, which is equivalent to a savings and loan in this country. His title is equivalent to a vice president for a savings and loan. Peter and his wife, Anne, and three-year-old Zachary live in Invercargill, a city of approximately 50,000 located on the southernmost tip of South Island.

Explaining that the main language they use at SBS is a UNISYS language called LINC, he chuckles, "Isn't it funny how we love to abbreviate things . . . like Y2K . . . mind you this abbreviation is what got us computer people into the dilemma in the first place isn't it?"

On Dec. 14, 1999, Heffernan said the SBS system was relatively free from Year 2000 issues.

"The media have suggested that the New Zealand government should have done more (especially in terms of educating the public on the problem), and even went as far as to suggest last year (1998) that the government systems might not be ready in time. This doesn't seem to have been mentioned this year (1999), so maybe the media were convinced by the government departments that things were better than the media thought."

As in the United States, Heffernan suggests the biggest concerns in New Zealand were its power supply and city services, such as water and sewage.

"We've had assurances that the local city councils don't think there will be trouble, but they are making no guarantees," he says. "The banks are running advertisements, telling people that their money is safe and to leave it in their accounts—not put it under the mattress. They are suggesting burglars will be out in force looking to steal the cash if left in the house."

North of Invercargill, on North Island, is the city of Palmerston North, the home of Alan and Lynne Krivan. The Krivans work for Harvey World Travel, an Australian based travel firm in this community of 75,000, which is north (where else?) of the capital city of Wellington.

The travel company changed its computers over as early as October of 1998, mostly because there were other problems, but at the same time brought them into the 21st Century.

"It appears all large organizations have prepared, such as banks, power companies, hospitals, etc., which has led us to believe they have all had test runs," states Lynne Krivan. "But our next-door neighbor works for Transpower, which is the public utility that runs the high voltage electricity transmission lines around New Zealand, and he has told us he is working New Year's Eve just in case," she adds.

"Radio and TV advertising is in the form of a cockroach (the representative for the Y2K bug) of all things, telling us to be ready for the change-over."

But for the optimistic in New Zealand, New Year's Eve is still party time.

"Kiwis love to party and New Year's Eve is usually the big one," states Anne Heffernan. *"In Invercargill we have a committee that has organized bands, fireworks displays, and there will be prize draws throughout the night, with a big prize at 5 a.m."*

In the little town of Riverton, where Anne grew up, it will be more like a carnival, with a variety of entertainment, including the Invercargill Pipe Band. At sunrise they will breakfast on the beach and have a hangi-food cooked the traditional Maori way, in the ground.

Besides the hangi, there will be games for all ages, including beach volleyball and tug-of-war.

And according to Anne Heffernan, "Law and order problems started early. Police were flat out in Queenstown (near the west coast of South Island) and Arrowtown (about 10 miles northeast of Queenstown). They are popular places to be at New Year for the late teens through early thirties." She adds, "The police were answering so many calls they were picking the more serious to attend and worrying about the rest later."

CHAPTER FOUR

If traveling is truly broadening,
Jane and I would each be four feet wide.

The year 2000 also included the first of an eventual two trips to Europe during the first decade of the new millennium. We were blessed with seventeen wonderful days touring Germany, Austria, Switzerland and Northern Italy.

We took in the Passion Play, a portrayal of the last week of Christ's life, at Oberammergau, Germany. The event is held only every ten years. We had heard of it and our travel agent, Kathy Arthur, was able to obtain tickets.

It was held in a huge amphitheater which seated 4,000 people. What a wonderful production. Even though we knew how it would end, it was still an emotion-filled drama. I was watching parts of it through binoculars, including where spikes were driven through Jesus' feet. Even through the glasses it looked every bit as though it was actually happening.

When it was over, Jane said she was too distraught to join the others in our party in a banquet room at our hotel. So we settled for a sidewalk café on one of the popular streets in Oberammergau.

That was a mistake. At around midnight that night Jane became terribly sick to her stomach. Making a long story short, the next night we were in Austria, where we spent half a day in a Vienna hospital. She was diagnosed with food poisoning

Fortunately, that was one of the rare places where we were going to spend two days. Obviously we missed several attractions and a night at the theatre, but after the medications given Jane at the hospital, she slept most of the two days and I was able to do our laundry in the hotel's laundromat.

Fortunately also, the large bus on which we toured was not completely full and at the back was one long bench-like seat where Jane could rest and sleep on occasion. Other than her illness, it was a wonderful trip. We even had our pictures taken with the Matterhorn in the background at Zermatt, Switzerland. In the foreground, was a Swiss flag which the photographer had placed in my hand and a stupid, lazy, sleepy-looking St. Bernard dog sitting in front of us. Like we wanted this adrenalin-pumped animal in the picture. But I suppose it did add to the ambiance of the moment.

Jane and I at the Matterhorn at Zermatt, Switzerland. Notice the pumped-up St. Bernard.

CHAPTER FIVE

*The best thing about traveling in a foreign country
is traveling in a foreign country.*

Two other events that year, on a more positive note, occurred for us also. David was the 4-H director for Michigan State University and had an office in the county building in Midland.

He had completed his master's degree at MSU, and called us with an urgent request. He stated that a group of Japanese youth was going to be placed in homes in the area for a month, and could we possibly house one of the Japanese adult counselors. We had never given that idea a thought, but we said we could do it. That was soon to be our introduction to the witty, wise and wonderful, Michiko Takahashi.

Michiko, 39, was fairly fluent in English as she taught the same to Japanese youth. In the short two weeks we learned to love her and showed her as much of Michigan as time allowed, including the Mackinac Bridge, Mackinaw Island and so she could get her passport stamped with another foreign country, we drove into Canada from Sault (Soo) Ste. Marie and spent a couple enjoyable hours in that country.

On the way back, we stopped in some gift shops in Mackinaw City. At one point, I asked Michiko if she saw something her husband, Yoshi (whom we had never as yet met), might like. I wanted to buy him something from me . . . man-to-man so to speak. She looked at me and in her broken English, said, "I will tell him you are hot." I appreciated that, but why would she tell her husband? It wasn't until later that I understood she was saying, "I will tell him you are a sweethot." The Japanese have trouble with their R's and their L's. You can imagine what most of them do with my first name, which contains three of them. But I've even had people in my own country cut it to ribbons, especially telemarketers who

13

are too anxious to make a sale to take time to reason it out. Anyway, I would rather a woman tell me I am "hot" and not tell her husband.

Michiko was so witty and funny. At times I would turn to Jane and jokingly say, "Can we keep her?" One dirty look followed another and I finally shut up.

Because we had participated in this exchange program, we were offered a nearly three-week trip to Japan that fall for the mere sum of $1900 each, which included round-trip airfare, a tour of various parts of the country and room and board. Even in 2001, that was a bargain.

The huge 747 lifted off the runway at the International Airport in Detroit, flew over a part of Alaska, and landed at Narita International in Tokyo 13 1/2 hours later. It was good that I had taken my laptop computer along as it gave me something to do. I began recording our experience.

I had been a resident of Japan back in the mid-50's as a member of the U.S. Army. When I bid farewell to the Land of the Rising Sun as our troop ship sailed out of Tokyo Bay, I never gave a thought as to the possibility of ever returning.

Yet, there we were. Jane and I, my bride of over 40 years, and the 747 out of Detroit was heading for the air over Anchorage, Alaska, before slipping down the other side of the globe and into Tokyo. What made the trip even more apprehensive was the fact that the day we left Detroit on this multi-thousand mile trip halfway around the world, it was exactly three weeks after terrorists committed those horrific tragedies in New York, Washington, D.C., and rural Pennsylvania.

Anyone who flies coach class knows that a full plane is a cramped plane. Thirteen-and-a-half hours later the crampiness can lead to ten hours of crabbiness. Some people's legs weren't made to retain the same position for that long. Neither is the upper torso. When the seat ahead of you is reclined to the max, there is about eight inches between you and the person's head in front of you. Jane and I made frequent trips up and down the aisle to relieve the muscle aches.

Arriving in Tokyo a half-hour later than the scheduled time, it was 6:00 p.m. the following day. We had gained a day crossing the International Dateline. It was a dreary, drizzly day, but as warm as it had been back in Detroit.

The plane came to a smooth landing and we entered another world. And because of the location of our seats, we were among the last people on the plane to reach Tokyo.

By bus we were transported to the Youth Olympic Center in Tokyo. The dormitory-like buildings were built to house athletes during the Summer Olympics of 1964. They are now being used for educational conferences and the like.

Saying the rooms were small would be an overstatement. And the fact that it was called the Olympic Center immediately told you for whom the building was intended. One floor was for males, and one for females. That included males and females who had slept together for over 40 years.

My room, on the third floor, consisted of a single bed, a small wastebasket, a table just large enough for my laptop computer and a glass of water, and a small vault in one corner. The bed was placed in another corner, and there were about two feet between it and the opposite wall.

With temperatures in the mid-70s, and the humidity much higher than that, the room was very stuffy. I went to open the single window, but there was a note on it, in both English and Japanese, which read, "Window is broken. Please don't touch." The note obviously came from a professional printing press and was attached to the glass with a permanent glue; the kind that comes on a new window from the manufacturer, telling you what a wonderful product you have just purchased, but not mentioned how to get the note off. The window wasn't meant to be opened!

The first week we were part of a group of Americans who were guided to fabulous sights of the country. Many of them were places where I had visited during my military days at Camp Zama in 1956-57 (the 20th year of my life). These included Mt. Fuji, the Giant Buddha Statue in Kamakura (built in 1492), and the Golden Pavilion in Kyoto (built in the 1300s).

I wished to visit my old Army base at Zama, but recent world events prevented it. *Perhaps next time,* I thought. I truly hoped there would be a "next time."

After a week of traveling with our group, we were placed on a train to Chiba, on the Chiba Peninsula, just south of Tokyo. We were to meet two delightful people; Nobu and Shimako Tomono. We didn't even know them until we reached their train station and there was Shimako, smiling, and waiting with a sign in her hands which read, "Thomas." That was the only clue as to whom we were to meet.

Nobu worked for a company in Japan that often sent him to the States on business. He was in California when we arrived so we didn't get to meet him until two days later. His English was good as was Shimako's as she also taught English to Japanese young people. Nobu was born in London and his family moved back to Japan during World War II. I never could understand why they would do that, except London was being bombed as well.

Shimako and Nobu Tomono with Jane on our back porch.

What a wonderful couple they were and we enjoyed them so much, even though, because they had no beds, we did have to sleep on mats on the floor.

We stayed with them for a week on the beautiful Chiba Peninsula.

We met many of their friends and saw many sights we would not have seen without their help, including Mt. Fuji. I had been to Mt. Fuji during my time in the Army in 1957 and it is an awesome mountain. It was nostalgic to see it once again . . . and not in a military uniform.

While we were in Kyoto, our Japanese guide approached us with airline tickets in hand. Michiko had purchased them and sent them to our guide to give to us. We had already planned to fly to their home in Fukushima, about 150 miles north of Tokyo, but these tickets as a gift were a bit much.

Michiko and Yoshi had a very small home so they had rented a cottage for the week in a resort just outside town. Yoshi was a self-employed carpenter, and had to work part of the week. He was also illiterate in

English, but had a smile, and used it often, to light a room. He and Michiko were a delightful couple.

It was at this resort that I had another taste of ancient Japanese culture. One evening Yoshi took me to an indoor spa where all the men stripped and soaked in a huge tub of hot water. Once was enough. I was still the only one there with white skin and got some dubious looks.

When we returned home I wrote a story of the trip, hoping to have it published in the *Midland Daily News*. However, it turned out to be twenty-one pages . . . a bit long for a newspaper story, and I didn't have the energy or inclination to shorten it or make it into several short stories.

But the full document still remains in booklet form in my files (titled *Japan in 2001* . . . now that's original), along with many other Nobel Peace Prize quality writings . . . Ok, leave out the "Nobel Peace Prize" quality. Or any prize for outstanding literature, as far as that goes.

CHAPTER SIX

*It's good to have goals even if you don't yet know
how to meet them.*

In 2001 came another very worthwhile event in our lives. We purchased a double-wide mobile home at Plantation Estates in beautiful Ft. Myers, Florida in March of that year. I don't know why they called them "mobile homes" because they certainly aren't mobile and once parked they don't even have wheels to make them mobile. But it had as many square feet as the home on Scott Street in Midland in which Brenda and Dave grew up. And I guess they call them "double wide" because they have twice as much space as a "single wide." Even a single wide mobile home, once parked, have the wheels removed.

We had rented, for three years, a unit in the area, including two years at Plantation Estates, so we knew if we ever settled in Florida away from the Michigan winters, that was where we wanted to be . . . mostly because that was where our good friends, Dave and Jan Weissenborn, had purchased a place and we had come to know many of the people who lived there, either permanent residents or people from the mid-west or New England states. It turned out to be one of the best decisions of our lives.

As soon as the ink had dried on the $70,000 purchase (the previous owner had originally asked $85,000), we invited Dave, Kathy, Stacy and Ashley to join us for spring break. We didn't tell them we had bought it and it was a complete surprise to them.

But they were excited just to be in Florida, away from the Michigan winter in late March-early April. In an e-mail on March 25, 2001, Stacy had written:

"Ahh, yes . . . as I look through my crystal ball, Stacy, I see . . . is that Ohio, no, that must be Tennessee . . . no, no, not that one either, why . . . . IT'S FLORIDA! (and in your very near future, too!)

"Thanks for the count-down Grandpa! I'm so excited! I can almost hear the shrimp and lobster calling my name. Almost. Honestly, it makes me have to pee just thinking about it. I can absolutely not wait! Love you both dearly past the moon, the sun, the big dipper, and Pluto!"

Love, Stacy

Stacy was only fifteen at the time and her reference to a bodily secretion was a total surprise. She was a very Christian young lady and before she turned twenty had done missionary work in Central America and South Africa.

In the meantime, I continued work on my book, *Silent Heroes*. I included in the book, interviews with combat veterans from World War II, Korea and Vietnam. Several of the stories I had written for the Midland Daily News years earlier, included a Midland County resident, Oscar Holstrom, who fought in the Bolshevik Revolution in 1918. It appeared in the paper on September 20, 1983, his 89th birthday.

The book, and the combat stories in the Midland Daily News, brought numerous accolades. One in particular came from Dot Hornsby, a well-respected individual in the community and a pilot herself. I have never met her, but her e-mail of September 29, 2002, read:

Dear Lowell,

Particularly enjoyed your article this Sunday (As of this writing I have no idea which article it was). *Fascinating! I do the Aviation Camp for kids in the summer at Barstow Airport and the past two years had members of the Greatest Generation who were pilots come in to talk with the kids—the young people enjoy it and are most respectful of these men.*

Thanks for doing these articles for the paper—good for all of us to read them and I am sure a big ego boost for the people you write about—you do a great job describing events.

Dot Hornsby

Back to the ego thingy!

In addition to working on the stories for the book, I was also working on acquiring people of some note to endorse it on the back cover. One such person was Tom Brokaw, a famous news reporter for NBC, who wrote *The Greatest Generation*, a compilation of stories about World War II combat veterans across the nation. And he received accolades from across the nation for his work.

It was from Brokaw that I received my inspiration and decided that I would limit my interviews just to Midland County veterans. Either Brokaw didn't give a rap about my work or perhaps didn't even receive the several stories from the book at his New York office. At any rate, I never heard from him.

One well-known author I did hear from was Stephen Ambrose, or rather from his wife. He was a noted author and historian who had written several books on World War II. The response I received came from his wife, Anne, who apparently served as his agent. In an e-mail (I had e-mailed him earlier. His e-mail address was in one of the many articles he had written for a magazine publication). She wrote:

> *Thank you for writing. While he's always flattered to be asked for endorsements, Dr. Ambrose is unable to take time away from his own research and writing. Please accept our best wishes. Anne Ambrose.*

Dr. Ambrose died a couple years after that.

But the ego got a positive jolt in May of 2001. I had apparently sent to Kevin, a story I had done for the *Midland Daily News*. Just wish I could now identify the story. At any rate, Kevin wrote:

Grandpa,

> *That article was awesome! Thank you for sending it to me! You are such a GREAT writer, Grandpa! I wish I could write as well as you!"* Then to toot his own horn (so to speak), he added, *"Tonight I have the very last class of driver's training. That means I am just one step closer to getting my license! I can't wait!*

Kevin thought I had a great way with words, but he didn't do badly himself. More than once he wrote me things that boosted my ego and made me want to do better. Following is another, received in December, 2001. (Actually, I enjoyed sharing with him things I had written because he was always so sincere in his praise).

Grandpa,

That article was great!! Some day I wish to have the same writing skills as you do. I do enjoy writing quite a lot and I get good literature grades. Thank you for letting me know that you had written that. In my U.S. history class right now we just finished learning a lot about World War II and how the Japanese would fight for all they were worth. I am taking this article into my history class tomorrow to share it with my fellow classmates. This is a great article! Thank you! Please tell Grandma I said hello.

Hugs and kisses,
Kevin.

P.S. I am so proud of you, Grandpa!

Sigh . . . when you're good, you're good. But at this point, I cannot recall which article he was referring to.

But out of all the accolades I received this year, one horrible, unthinkable, unimaginable event startled the world, placing any praise I had received far, far into the background.

The headline in the *Midland Daily News,* in extra large, bold print read, "UNDER ATTACK." It was September 11, 2001.

Terrorists had hijacked four commercial jets and commandeered them into three national landmarks, and another into the foothills of Pennsylvania. It was theorized, and later proven, that the fourth landmark was intended to hit the White House in Washington, D.C. It was also theorized that a fight had broken out in the cockpit, causing the airliner to go down in a field in Pennsylvania.

All of us remember where we were and what we were doing when tragedy strikes. Jane was in Midland and I was preparing to take our boat out of the water for the winter. Our neighbor, Terry Siemienkiewicz (don't ask me to pronounce it. I think he's French or something), was going to drive our GMC Jimmy with the boat trailer to the pick-up point, and I would meet him there with the boat.

When Terry arrived in the yard, he asked if I had been watching TV. When I responded in the negative, he said, "A plane has been hi-jacked and slammed into the World Trade Center."

About that same time, Barbara Serrell, our neighbor across the lagoon called to ask if we were watching television. Barb was a teacher at a parochial school in Gladwin and was home with a bad cold.

Terry and I rushed into the house and turned on the TV and before our eyes, the second plane hit the second tower of the WTC. It was unbelievable! President George W. Bush declared it was war, not only on America, but on all freedom-loving countries. He hastened to say that not only would the guilty parties be caught and punished, but those harboring them would receive the same treatment.

Many newsmen equated this with Pearl Harbor with one exception; at Pearl we had a return address.

At this moment in history we didn't know for certain who the guilty parties were or where they could be found.

Later we began receiving e-mails from friends we had met from around the world. The first was from Michiko, our dear friend from Japan. She wrote:

> *The tragedy is broadcasting on all channels since yesterday. I am so sad. Words cannot convey how sad I am.*
>
> *Michiko*

Another note from friends, Lynne and Alan Krivan, in New Zealand said:

> *Words cannot express how one feels about the terrible waste of human life all because of some people. Is nobody allowed to have views on things these days? It seems not.*
> *I trust that you didn't have any family in any of the areas that were devastated.*

We saw the terrible events on TV last night. I could not sleep because a daughter of my English Club's member lives in NY. She lives near the twin towers.

I hate terrorists. They killed innocent people wholesale. We watched, stunned, at 6:30 this morning. It was like watching a horrible movie. You cannot ever replace the people who were just in the wrong place at the wrong time. Let us know how you all are.

I will e-mail again on the 26th September unless I hear from you before tomorrow morning.

Chin up. Look after yourselves and your fellow Americans.

God Bless you all.

Lynne and Alan

Also from New Zealand, and our good friends Vivian and Mike Spriggs, came this message:

Our prayers are for you and your fellow countrymen who are enduring this dreadful horror. It is just unbelievable but it has happened. Words cannot express how we feel other than to say, "The Lord be with you all at this most dreadful time."

We have not moved from the television all day as we have watched the tragedy unfold. September 12th will never be forgotten. (It was actually September 12 in New Zealand because they are on the other side of the International Date Line). *All our love,*

Viv and Mike.

A columnist for the Miami Herald, Leonard Pitts Jr., summed up brilliantly, what most Americans were thinking about the situation. I copy it here in total because it was such a brilliant essay. It was titled, *We'll Go Forward From this Moment:*

It's my job to have something to say. They pay me to provide words that help make sense of that which troubles the American soul. But in this moment of airless shock when hot tears sting disbelieving eyes, the only thing I can find to say, the only words that seem to fit, must be addressed to the unknown author of this suffering.

You monster. You beast. You unspeakable bastard.

What lesson did you hope to teach us by your coward's attack on our World Trade Center, our Pentagon, us? What was it you hoped we would learn?

Whatever it was, please know that you failed. Did you want us to respect your cause? You just damned your cause. Did you want to make us fear? You just steeled our resolve. Did you want to tear us apart? You just brought us together.

Let me tell you about our people. We are a vast and quarrelsome family, a family rent by racial, social, political and class division, but a family nonetheless. We're frivolous, yes, capable of expending tremendous emotional energy on pop cultural minutiae—a singer's revealing dress, a ball team's misfortune, a cartoon mouse.

We're wealthy too, spoiled by the ready availability of trinkets and material goods, and maybe because of that, we walk through life with a certain sense of blithe entitlement. We are fundamentally decent, though—peace-loving and compassionate. We struggle to know the right thing and to do it. And we are, the overwhelming majority of people of faith, believers in a just and loving God.

Some people—you, perhaps—think that any or all of this makes us weak. You're mistaken. We are not weak. Indeed, we are strong in ways that cannot be measured by arsenals.

Yes, we're in a pan now. We are in mourning and we are in shock. We're still grappling with the unreality of the awful thing you did, still working to make ourselves understand that this isn't a special effect from some Hollywood blockbuster, isn't the plot development from a Tom Clancy novel. Both in terms of the awful scope of their ambition and the probable final death toll, your attacks are likely to go down as the worst acts of terrorism in the history of the United States and, probably, the history of the world. You've bloodied us as we have never been bloodied before.

But there's a gulf of difference between making us bloody and making us fall. This is the lesson Japan was taught to its bitter sorrow the last time anyone hit us this hard, the last time anyone brought us such abrupt and monumental pain. When roused, we are righteous in our outrage, terrible in our force. When provoked by this level of barbarism, we will bear any suffering, pay any cost, go to any length, in the pursuit of justice.

I tell you this without fear of contradiction. I know my people, as you, I think, do not. What I know reassures me. It also causes me to tremble with dread of the future.

In the days to come, there will be recrimination and accusation, fingers pointing to determine whose failure allowed this to happen and what can be done to prevent it from happening again. There will be heightened security, misguided talk of revoking basic freedoms. We'll go forward from this moment sobered, chastened, sad. But determined, too. Unimaginable determined.

You see, the steel in us is not always readily apparent. That aspect of our character is seldom understood by people who don't know us well. On this day, the family's bickering is put on hold.

As Americans we will weep, as Americans we will mourn, and as Americans, we will rise in defense of all that we cherish.

So I ask again: What was it you hoped to teach us? It occurs to me that maybe you just wanted us to know the depths of your hatred. If that's the case, consider the message received. And take this message in exchange:

You don't know my people. You don't know what we're capable of. You don't know what you just started.

But you're about to learn.

Pitts was right about at least one thing . . . heightened security. Things have never been the same since at airports around the world. Beginning almost immediately after September 11, 2001, airport security personnel began examination of all luggage; sometimes by hand and other times by x-ray machines. Often people were asked to remove their shoes and belts as they passed through the security checks. And sometimes they were physically searched via a wand or by hand.

CHAPTER SEVEN

We don't have to look for enemies; they will always be there.

Our trip to Japan began just three weeks after 9/11. When we landed in Fukushima, the home of our dear friends Michiko and Yoshi, on a flight from Osaka, a police officer stopped Jane and I just as we were about to leave the airport with them.

He wanted to know who we were, where we were going and how long we would be staying. Of course, Michiko had to interpret for us. He also asked to see our passports. Later I mentioned to Jane that we were stopped for one of three reasons: 1) We were the only non-Japanese on the plane, 2) I was the only one on the plane with a beard (in other words we were "profiled," a dirty word that Muslims and Blacks used frequently after being stopped at airports), or 3) The officer had to inflate his nightly report that he had done something to aid his country.

When we left Japan, our flight from Tokyo stopped in Minneapolis/ St. Paul and we had to transfer to another plane for our trip to Midland. When we entered the concourse we had to wonder if our plane had been hijacked and we had landed somewhere in an obscure Middle-eastern country.

All over the place there were men in military uniform carrying guns. That's how bleak the situation was.

A few years later, in Frankfort, Germany, we had to go through the, now normal, security check <u>twice</u> before being allowed to enter the embarking area. At the second security check, the security guards appeared extra cautious as our gear was being transported on the moving belt through the x-ray machine.

Two months before we began our Japan journey Jane had had knee surgery and had borrowed a collapsible cane. It was going through the x-ray when the attendant stopped the belt and was looking at it on the screen. In German (after all, we were in Germany), he beckoned other guards to view it. I ducked my head around so I could see the monitor and realized his hesitation.

I picked up the cane (I can't imagine what was going through their heads at the time, and later thought that mine wasn't on particularly straight either, considering what could have been the consequences).

I disconnected the three parts of the cane to show them the expandable cable inside that held it together when extended. They, and we, were visibly relieved.

I have never resented having all the security checks at airports, but I will <u>always</u> resent those who have made them necessary.

CHAPTER EIGHT

*A truly great friend is hard to find, difficult to leave
and impossible to forget.*

2002 was a most unusual year. During the winter months we enjoyed
the beaches of Southwest Florida, and renovated our newly purchased
double-wide mobile home in south Ft. Myers. It was located near the
Gulf of Mexico in a park named, "Plantation Estates." It was a wonderful
reprieve from the harsh winters of Michigan. We would go there in
mid-December and return to our "real" home the end of April.

Previous to returning in April that year, we had made arrangements to
stop in Asheville, North Carolina. There we met Colonel Robert Morgan,
the pilot of the famous *Memphis Belle,* the first B-17 to fly 25 missions
over Europe without a casualty. He later led the first B-29 mission over
Tokyo. The Colonel was 84 years old, retired, and working full-time for a
real estate agent. He was also in perfect health. I was thrilled beyond belief.
I also wrote a story about our meeting for the *Midland Daily News.*

At the time I was working on my book, *Silent Heroes,* and after telling
the Colonel about it, he agreed to endorse it. Unfortunately, he never got
to see the book because he died prior to its arrival on the book stands.

But I wrote him a note of gratitude on October 31, 2002 that said:

Dear Colonel Morgan,

> *For a guy who bombed the hell out of two continents, you are a very
> unselfish and kind individual. I have received your generous endorsement
> for my upcoming book, and with it goes my undying gratitude, Sir.*
> *Thank you again for all your consideration. I am truly grateful to
> have become acquainted with another 'Silent Hero.'*

I hope Linda's recovery will be rapid and complete. (His wife was also going through the cancer thing the same time as Jane). *Our prayers and blessings to her. Jane is doing well and we are hoping she has had her final chemotherapy. We will know for certain next week.*

All the best to you both,
Lowell

CHAPTER NINE

Into every life some rain must fall.
We don't always know when it will be a thunderstorm.

The call came on Tuesday, July 2, 2002. Jane had been visiting doctors since the previous May, after arriving home from our four-month winter reprieve in Ft. Myers.

By the expression on her face, I knew the news was not good. Especially when she began tearing up. Our lives were about to forever change, or so we thought.

The prior February she had had a breast biopsy in Ft. Myers as the result of some unusual cells showing up on her annual mammogram. The biopsy proved negative. We had had many anxious moments leading up to that diagnoses and we were greatly relieved. Her doctor in Midland received a copy of her mammogram, and suggested she have a four-month follow-up mammogram when she arrived back home.

That x-ray also suggested some abnormal cells of the same breast, but in a different location. Further tests proved them to be cancerous. More anxious moments, but that incident in Florida undoubtedly saved her life. Had it not been for the follow-up exam (which would not have been called for had she not had that biopsy in February), the cancer would have been growing until the following December when she was scheduled for her next annual physical exam. All we could think of was, "He works in mysterious ways."

Stacy, then 16, and Ashley, 14, were with us when the call came in, and all four of us were in tears following that fateful telephone call. An appointment was set with Dr. Reif the following day at 11:00 a.m.

I had planned to take notes at that meeting, but since I had been interviewing people for the *Midland Daily News* for the past 30 years, I knew that many of the details of an interview came out only if they were recorded. So I took with me the small tape recorder, and asked Dr. Reif if he would mind if I took notes *and* taped our discussion. It was then that I realized how much shock I was in. As I tried to ask about recording, I broke into tears. I quickly got myself under control, however, but I didn't apologize for my feelings, nor did Dr. Reif or Jane make me feel as though I had done anything out of the ordinary. But it was out of the ordinary for me, and I was mildly embarrassed.

We were traumatized. For the next several days the tears would come from nowhere, and just as quickly subside. So many thoughts go through one's mind at those times. But Jane and I convinced ourselves that we would focus on the positive. Even the following Sunday on the way to church, Jane mentioned the pretty flowers growing in the ditch beside the road. That's how focused she was on the positive.

At the same time, Jane was being treated for skin cancer on her forehead. She had had a patch removed near the hairline, and had just completed ten x-ray treatments on another spot. Now that cancer had shown up in her breast, one of my burning questions was, *how many other places in her body were harboring these murderous cells?*

Surgery was scheduled for July 11. Brenda sat with me in the hospital waiting room while Jane was being prepared for surgery. Dave would have been with us as well except he had previously arranged business out of state, and Jane and I insisted he keep the appointment. Actually, I had hoped to wait by myself . . . until it was over . . . it was then I realized how important it was to have family and friends with me in those times.

Jane, Brenda and I had been through a two-hour meeting the day before, with a team of nurses who would be involved in the whole process, plus a one-hour meeting with the surgeon. From what we learned, we were greatly encouraged. It looked like the cancer cells were pretty much localized, but they wouldn't know until the surgeon got in to have a look at the lymph nodes.

Time began to drag by. Jane was wheeled in her hospital bed to the pre-op room about 11:30 a.m. Brenda and I went to the hospital cafeteria for some lunch. Shortly after noon, Kathy (our daughter-in-law) came in, got some lunch and sat with us. The conversation was solemn, none of us smiling much, and most of the time avoiding the subject of cancer.

We had taken our lunch trays to an open-air verandah, where we sat at a round stone table shaded by large maples. We hadn't sat there long when we looked up and saw one of Jane's best friends, Sandie Butler, walk up to us. She had already had lunch, but would wait with us.

Following lunch, the four of us headed back to the waiting room for a long afternoon. At three o'clock, the surgeon, Dr. Reif, came into the waiting room. *Oh good, it's over,* I thought. But it hadn't yet begun. The surgeon walked over to someone else to inform them of the results of his early afternoon.

Jane's surgery was scheduled for 2:30, but a half-hour later it hadn't started. We realized it would be a still longer day. We didn't know why the schedule was so backed up until we heard Jane's explanation in her hospital room following surgery.

For surgery of this type, it is necessary to insert radioisotopes, in the form of a liquid, into the veins in the breast. The technician then follows these isotopes on a computer screen as they wind their way through the lymph nodes. The surgeon then has no trouble finding the nodes, and those he wishes to remove.

One problem, however. The isotopes were not cooperating. They were staying where they had been inserted into the breast, not moving at all. An hour-and-a-half went by. The technician called Dr. Reif on the phone, giving him the update on the isotopes. Dr. Reif said to give them another half-hour.

Jane related to me later that, in tears, she prayed to God to make her body cooperate, and moments later both she and the technician saw the dark blue sketches of the isotopes as they moved along the vein from the breast to the lymph nodes. Nearly two hours had passed since the first attempt had been made to accomplish this task.

The hours dragged, and those of us concerned wondered why. Around 4:30 p.m. the phone in the waiting room rang, and the party asked for me. *At last,* I thought, *it's over, and the doctor is on his way out.*

Not so. A nurse in the operating room called to say the surgery should be over within a half-hour or so and briefly explained the delay in terms I didn't particularly understand. Or perhaps I was too numb with anxiety to comprehend.

Kathy had had to leave because Stacy was preparing to take her driver's test so she could hopefully get her license. (We later learned she had past with flying colors. Stacy had also had a stressful day).

Brenda, Sandie and I waited another hour before Dr. Reif made his appearance. He first apologized for the lengthy delay, and then stated that the surgery had gone well, that he had removed an area about the size of a large egg from Jane's left breast, plus three of her lymph nodes. He mentioned that since the first three (each person has between 10 and 20 of them on each side, according to Dr. Reif), were not affected, there was no reason to remove any more.

Pathology later revealed the removed lymph nodes were, indeed, clean. But that fact did not end our worry and anxiety.

Almost two weeks later to a day, July 24, Jane and I met with Dr. Reif in his office to go over the results of the pathology report and to have her stitches removed. She would forever carry about a three-inch scar under her arm where the lymph nodes were removed, and a four-inch scar on her left breast.

Dr. Reif could not, in all honesty, state whether or not Jane would need extended chemotherapy, but 5-6 weeks of radiation on the breast was a given. The sessions would be 15 minutes, five days a week. If chemotherapy was needed, however, that would have to come first.

The office had already made an appointment with Dr. Hurtubise, an oncologist, to make the determination on chemo. It was not to be his determination, however, it was ours. He explained that there were two stages of cancer. In stage one, chemo is not necessarily recommended. In stage two, it is. Jane's was about a one-and-a-half. Chemo would increase the odds of cancer showing up again by only three to five percent. We alone would have to make the determination. But we liked the odds.

It was Thursday, July 25. Dr. Hurtubise suggested we think it over during the weekend. By the next day, Jane had already decided. She had talked on the phone with close friends, Marje and Don Abbott, whose son was an oncologist in Washington, D.C. Jane had also talked with him regarding the pathology report.

The bottom line was, why wouldn't anyone want to do everything possible to increase their odds against cancer? Even three to five percent odds? The decision was made. Jane would have chemotherapy.

She called Hurtubise's office on Friday morning to inform him of her decision. The good doctor was not in that day, so her response would have to wait until Monday. Waiting, at that point, was the worst part. The decision had been made, so let's move on and get this nasty procedure behind us. We couldn't leave the house or even make lengthy phone calls because we so much wanted to receive his call.

Finally, Jane made another call to his office on Monday and asked to talk to a nurse who might clue her in as to the procedure of getting started, and perhaps even when we might begin. The nurse was busy, but would return the call. She didn't. More frustration.

We had wanted to leave for Midland and Saginaw on Monday to look for a wig for the inevitable. On Tuesday morning Jane once more called the doctor's office on the chance that either the doctor or a nurse might be available at that time. They weren't, and Jane asked if the nurse might return the call after 4:00 that afternoon. She would.

Jane and I left for the Midland County Cancer Society office to look for a possible used wig. Often, as people purchase them, and after using them, they return them to the office for someone else to use. Jane picked out two possibilities, along with several turbans and scarves that have become well known to cancer patients. She was allowed to bring them home to "try them out." Jane confessed to me that she was very uncomfortable with all this. Little wonder.

The Cancer Society also encourages patients to go to a hairdresser in Saginaw who handles new wigs. Armed with instructions on how to find the shop, we headed out.

Jane knew as soon as she tried one of the many on, that it was a right fit for her. The color would have to be ordered, and would be in within a week, but at least no one would walk down the street, look at her hair, and say to themselves, *There's my wig.* Somehow that was important to Jane, and I understood. Now she was ready for chemo and the devastation we knew it would wreak on her hair.

Even before Jane's hair began falling out, I told her that when her hair comes back in I hoped it will be blond because they are supposed to have more fun, and I wanted to be a part of that action. I can think positive too.

Going to Saginaw, however, had a three-pronged motive. The second was to have lunch at Red Lobster, which we both loved. The third was to look at the possibility of purchasing a second computer. The new one would be used for the Internet, and the old one for my writing. Jane and I could both use a computer at the same time.

Before leaving for Saginaw I had researched the Gateway web site, found the "bargain of the week," printed it off and marched into the

Gateway store, asking if we could get it for the same price as on the web site. The answer was what we wanted to hear, and we now had a state of the art computer to replace the seven-year-old clunker that had been so faithful to us. It became "mine" while the new one, of course, would be Jane's. The computer store had none in stock, but promised delivery the following week.

We felt good about our day. Getting the computer helped dissolve some of the depression Jane was feeling, knowing that very soon she would have no hair of her own.

Arriving home about 4:15, we found two messages on the answering machine. One was from Dr. Hurtubise. He had been returning Jane's call from the previous Friday. Obviously he had not been informed that we would not be available until after 4:00 p.m. He stated he would call later in the day.

I was working in the yard when Jane came out. Dr. Hurtubies had just called and Jane was to begin chemotherapy on the following Friday morning, August 9, 2002.

We clutched at each other, and both began to weep. "Why are we crying?" I asked between sobs. "This is what we have wanted, to get it started."

"I know," Jane sniffled, and we both began to laugh.

That evening we sat in our hot tub on the screened-in porch, and watched the mercurochrome-colored water of the lake turn to shades of purple, then black until the sun was only a smile on the horizon . . . then darkness.

The next two days were torturous for Jane. She worked around the house and cooked dishes to be frozen as though she was nine months pregnant. I worked around the yard and on my writing. I also prepared and mailed a manuscript to Colonel Morgan. It was a stressful 48 hours.

CHAPTER TEN

No one is in charge of your happiness but you.

Friday finally arrived like a snake crawling lazily in the grass. Slowly. Somehow deadly. Our apprehension, on a scale of one to ten, was off the chart. Never had we suffered so slowly, nor agonized so adamantly.

Dr. Hurtubise, a wonderful man, with a kind and honest heart in his 50's did his best to help us relax, but the butterflies in the gut were definitely not flying in formation.

He began by inserting a tube, called a "central line port," just below Jane's collarbone, and into an artery just above the heart. He attached the port to her skin with two stitches, as it would remain in place the whole time she was to be taking her chemo treatments. Her six treatments, it was believed, would be two to three weeks apart, and that would take us almost to Christmas.

After the port was in place, Jane was taken to x-ray to make certain it was in the correct position. The reason for the tube leading to the heart, we learned, was because the top of the heart has the most pressure, and the chemotherapy drugs were so potent that they had to be distributed to the rest of the body as rapidly as possible to avoid damage to any part of the body.

After determining that the port was correctly placed, Jane was wheeled to the oncology department and her first treatment began. This first one was a lengthy one, and we had spent a total of five hours at the hospital before we were ready to leave for home.

Before we did, however, and after the chemo had dripped into her heart for about one and a half hours, the nurse attached a small pump filled with another drug fitted in a belly bag which would be working for the next four days. This drug was so lethal that it dripped the equivalent of only two drops per hour, 24-hours per day.

Before leaving the hospital, we both watched a short video about how to change the dressing over the port, and I had a crash course on actually doing it. That had to be done weekly for the four months the port would be in place. It was quite a procedure, particularly when everything had to remain sterile. (I didn't tell them I had been sterile for the past thirty years).

The belly bag was very uncomfortable for Jane, difficult to sleep with, and awkward to shower with as I had to hold the pump above the shower door as she bathed. But it would be only for four days at a time, two to three weeks apart.

The weekend went by without incident, but by Monday morning Jane had severe symptoms of nausea. The prescription she took from the doctor's office on Friday was priced at $828 for thirty pills. That's nearly $28 a pop, and she had been popping them at the rate of three per day. I was only too happy to fork over our $20 co-pay for the pills. But they weren't working!

Fortunately we had a doctor's appointment that afternoon, and she got another medication for nausea (this one only $37). The combination of the two pills worked. Upon arriving home, Jane slept for two hours, then after another pill at bedtime, she got a good night's sleep.

Two weeks later, the inevitable began to occur. Jane's hair began to leave its traces all over the house and in the bed. For a week she had been psyching herself up for this, and now was the time. She would say things like, "I've never seen my scalp. That should be interesting," and "I wonder what it will be like to wash the top of my head with a wash cloth?" In her positive frame of mind, she said it would be just one more step behind us, and nearer the end of this whole mess, and that it had to be done.

She got out an old oil cloth table cover, placed it on the bathroom floor, leaned over it, and handed me the electric clippers, saying, "Don't you dare cry!" I didn't, but I was close. She didn't either. She did avoid, however, looking in the mirror for several minutes. But when she finally did, she said, "Think of all the shampoo I'm going to save over the next four months." Always the optimist.

The wig was a perfect match, and I told Jane that if people didn't know, they just wouldn't know. She became comfortable with it, but she still wore the turbans around the house.

Three weeks later came chemo treatment number two. While waiting for Jane to receive treatment, I attended a doctor's appointment for my annual physical examination, and learned I had a hernia behind my belly button. For 66 years an "inny," now I was an "outty." The doc said he could line me up with a surgeon, or I could just let it go, hoping it wouldn't get worse. I chose the latter. We didn't need anymore operations this year.

Chemo number two meant we were one-third through the horrid treatments. While we knew what to expect by now, Jane wasn't prepared for the terrible mouth sores we knew were imminent. At one point our conversations were more like a game of charades. Her tongue and mouth were so painful, she couldn't talk without near collapse. I would try to converse so she could answer with only a nod of the head. For example, when I would ask her where she put something, I would say, "Let me put that another way, 'Did you put it in the hall closet?'" She could then respond with a nod.

During this time, my emotional pain was only slightly less than her physical pain. When in prayer, whether by myself or in a church group, and Jane was mentioned, I broke down in sobs. I soon learned not to volunteer a prayer in a group.

Her mouth sores continued throughout the week, and finally on Friday, she called Dr. Hurtubise's office and got another prescription for the sores and for the pain. She slept most of Saturday after swallowing the pain killer. At least when she was asleep she couldn't feel the pain.

One evening that week we had a surprise visit from two old friends from church and from our old neighborhood on the lake, Brad and Sherri Snow. We hadn't seen or heard from them for at least two years, and the shock of seeing their situation helped our spirits, but not Jane's pain. Sherri had had a heart attack a year earlier, taking her out of the labor force, which greatly reduced their income. She now had head tremors that forced her to cup her face in her hands while she talked.

Brad, who had 27 years with his employer, was about to be down-sized out of a job, and they were about to lose their house on the lake due to the loss of Sherri's job. And we thought we had problems!

But Jane's mouth sores persevered. I felt as helpless as a lamb being led to slaughter. Nothing I did could cheer her up. One morning as I was working in the yard, I looked through the office window, and saw her sitting there with her back to me, playing a game of Backgammon with someone somewhere in the world on the Internet. I cocked my cap at a weird angle, tapped on the glass pane, and made a funny face. She turned around, gave a weak wave with one hand, and an even weaker smile, and returned to her game. It had been nearly a week since I had seen her smile.

After she had suffered like this for eight days, I finally called Doctor Hurtubise's office to ask if there wasn't *something* more they could do. It was the doctor's day to be in another city, and all the nurse could do was tell us to go to ER, and if they thought it serious enough, they could get in touch with Hurtubise. The only answer we got in ER was, "You are using every medication we would suggest. We really can't think of anything else." That was no cheering thought either.

In the meantime the cards and phone calls kept pouring in, some from people we had had no contact with for years. People out there were concerned.

On August 18, two days before Jane was to receive her third chemo treatment, and two days after our 44th wedding anniversary, she had an appointment with Dr. Hurtubise. It was decided not to have her treatment that week, but to wait for the sores in her mouth to completely heal. It might take a week, and it was pretty much her call.

Hurtubise also decided to administer the chemo a little differently in order to help avoid the mouth sores. She would no longer use the belly bag pump after the treatments, but rather, it would be infused in the office with the other chemicals. We didn't understand how that could possibly help, and we were apprehensive going into her next treatment, whenever that would be. But at least the next treatment would put us half-way through the therapy, with three more treatments to go.

The third treatment was postponed by just a week, to September 27, 2002. For the first day-and-a-half all was fine. In fact, much of Saturday she spent in the kitchen, baking and whatever else she loves doing in the kitchen. That was a good sign. On Sunday morning we were on our way to the Methodist church in Clare. Stacy and Ashley were performing an interpretive dance with other girls from their church that morning. On the way there, Jane mentioned she was getting sleepy. I told her to go ahead and sleep in church, that I wouldn't wake her up. I'd just let her lay there. She smiled and drifted off.

Well, she didn't sleep in church. But she slept all the way home, and most of the rest of the day. In the meantime, Dave had been here the day before, helping me put away the summer toys, cutting overhanging limbs, etc. So Sunday afternoon I cleaned the paddle boat, ready to put it in the pole barn, and brought up some fire wood for the days that were sure to cool down. But the helpless feeling began creeping back in once again.

The sleepiness was easy to deal with, and by the beginning of the second week Jane was feeling so well that we planned a few days' trip to the Upper Peninsula.

We started off with an overnight in Grayling staying with our good friends, Dave and Jan Weissenborn. It was a lovely stay; grilled pork chops for dinner, good conversation and several hands of Euchre that wasn't so good for Dave and me.

The following morning we drove over to near Traverse City to visit friends we had met in our mobile home park in Florida, Bill and Sue Carter.

We had made arrangements to meet with the publisher I was planning to use for my book in early afternoon in Traverse City. It went well, and we were encouraged by the meeting.

Then we headed north, across the Mackinac Bridge, and into St. Ignace where we stayed the night and played the noisy machines at the casino. At the motel we were each given coupons worth ten dollars in gold-colored coins to use at the casino. We were also given the same amount of coupons for the following day.

We exchanged the coupons for coins at the casino and managed to lose them all. Jane asked me for $20, I reluctantly gave her $10, and within seconds that was gone as well.

We left the smoked-filled casino, deciding not to return to even use the coupons/coins the next day.

It was I, however, the following morning who suggested we return to the casino just long enough to use the coupons/coins. If we lose we haven't lost *our* money, and if we win, we simply come out ahead. It was strange that I would even think this way because I am not fond of casinos, or anywhere else where people so willingly lose shirts they may not have.

By the time all the coins had made their way to the bottom of the machines, we had won quarters worth $76.50. We cashed in, but Jane dropped the .50 in the machines on the way to the door. I was just happy the $76 was in bills.

We then headed west. Our plan was to drive US-2 along the top of Lake Michigan over to Bay de Noc, spend the night, and head for home the next day. We drove as far (88 miles said the road sign) to Manistique in a pouring rain. Undaunted, Jane shopped a Ben Franklin store on Main Street, and we decided we had had enough of the UP. We hopped in the Park Avenue and headed back west toward St. Ignace. We didn't stop there, however, but crossed the Mighty Mackinac Bridge and got a hotel room on the lake in Mackinaw City.

The rain had stopped, and the turning leaves on the maple trees were near their prime. It was early October. And we had enjoyed leaving home, if even for a few days.

The following morning we packed up and began the three-hour drive down along I-75. We were just north of Harrison, about 45 minutes from home when Jane said, "I don't think I packed my wig." (She had put on one of her colorful head scarves for travel). I pulled off on the shoulder, which isn't necessarily a safe thing to do on an international highway. But this was a week day, and the traffic was light.

She searched the trunk and back seat, and confirmed her feelings. The wig was still on the tall post of the four-poster bed in Mackinaw City . . . unless an unwitting room attendant put it in her pocket to complete her Halloween costume three weeks hence.

While I unpacked the car at home, Jane called the motel, and indeed the wig was there. They agreed to send it priority mail, and Jane would have it the next day. We were greatly relieved. But Jane wouldn't be wearing it for another week.

The next morning the ugly ravages of the chemo kicked in. I left the house at 8:00 a.m. to have breakfast with the ROMEO Club (Retired Old Men Eating Out) just three miles away. I arrived home shortly after nine, and Jane was still in bed. I let her sleep until 11:30. When she got up she had chills and felt warm at the same time. She had a temperature of just over 100. It rose even slightly more as the day wore on.

She was supposed to have a blood test that day anyway, so on the way we stopped at the oncologist's office. The doctor was doing his thing in a neighboring town, so the nurse advised us to go to the Emergency Room.

During our six-hour stay in ER, they took her blood for testing, and gave her a drip bag of some solution which took a half-hour. Never once did they ask Jane if she was comfortable, would like to use the rest room, or how she was feeling. I helped myself to a blanket in the cupboard in the room and covered her. I stifled what I was thinking as I observed a half-dozen doctors and numerous nurses parading through the area attending to no more than two or three patients in those long six hours.

Finally Jane was admitted and was told she would be in the hospital for three to seven days. The atmosphere in her new room was that of caring and compassion, much unlike her stay in ER.

Her temperature was nearly103 by this time, and they had two drip bags going simultaneously; one was antibiotics and another, a saline solution (I think) that would keep her from dehydrating.

People who came to call on her for the next four days had to first wash their hands thoroughly before touching her. I went to the hospital each day and sat through long hours while she drifted in and out of sleep. Finally I took my lap top computer with me and worked on chapters of my book, *Silent Heroes,* in her room.

Helplessness continued to creep its ugly head into my gut once more, but I was more concerned about Jane who just lay there trying to gain enough strength to come back home. By her third day, she was beginning to feel better, and in her hospital bed was looking up addresses of the veterans I had interviewed, so I could send them a mailing.

The cards and flowers poured in, but it was a long four days. Jane arrived home tired, but happy to be where she should be once again.

Two days later she had a previously planned appointment with Dr. Hurtubise. This would also determine whether or not she was in condition to receive her scheduled chemo two days after that. And even if she was, we were both dreading it.

We knew God wouldn't hand us anything we couldn't handle. We just wish He didn't have so much confidence in us.

And as always, sweet, sweet Michiko kept sending her frequent, encouraging e-mails from Japan. One dated July 2, 2002 said, in part,

> *It is good you received the green tea* (which she had sent earlier) *It is really good for health. I know you do not like strong tea (you drink it in Tokyo . . . it was the color of pea soup without peas), so I sent you green tea with sugar. You like it or not?*
>
> *You went to the doctor today, didn't you? I hope the cancer has gone. You need radiation treatment? Is it easy? You told us do not worry, but we*

really worry about you. We always PRAY for YOU. (Being Buddhists, they undoubtedly prayed to Buddha).
I hope you will be okay soon.

Love and xoxoxoxoxo
Michiko

On August 8, 2002, Michiko sent yet another note that said,

Lowell, we pray for Jane every day. We hope she will recover soon. I sent a charm for recovery on Monday. Please hand it to her it. We love you both very much.

Michiko and Yoshi

Another e-mail we received from dear friends in New Zealand, which read,

It has been hard to make myself write to you. It is easier to not accept and try and push your last e-mail away.
I feel shattered . . . .
How must you two be feeling? Our prayers of healing and protection for you are constantly before the Father.
It is such scary stuff . . . . BUT.
We must always remember our refuge and strength, our ROCK, in whom we trust.
Please know we love you guys heaps.

Love from us,
Viv and Mike

CHAPTER ELEVEN

Having surgery is like wanting to be on the other side of the mountain,
but not wanting to go through the tunnel to get there.

The appointment went well, and we heard the best news we had
received in a long time. Four chemo treatments may be all Jane would
need! But we wouldn't know for certain until we met with Hurtubise
again in three weeks. And she would be able to get number four in just
two days as originally scheduled.

Number four came and went well. In addition, they gave Jane a
prescription for helping the bone marrow grow the good blood cells faster,
thus trying to keep her out of the hospital. It was in the form of four
shots which I could give her at home. I was used to giving Jane shots of
methotrexate for her arthritis once a week prior to her receiving chemo
treatments. The price of the four shots was just under $1900! Part of the
cost was for paying for the national publicity on television. Why don't
the drug companies take that money and spend it on research and let the
doctors do the prescribing? But I was only too happy to fork over our
$20 co-pay on our insurance. Little wonder Medicare and some insurance
companies are in deep doo-doo.

Our jubilant attitudes after knowing she might have had her last
chemo treatment, however, dissipated a tad when, on the way home, we
hit a deer coming out of a ditch and crossing the road. Nothing $2000
wouldn't fix. Insurance companies can be good things!

After Jane's first chemo treatment, Brenda had arranged with a
florist in Beaverton to deliver flowers after her next three treatments,
but that I would call them first so the timing would be right. After her
fourth treatment, and after the shot of the expensive stuff, she didn't
have the usual symptoms so I didn't call. I decided that the flowers will

be a "congratulations" gift from Brenda after Jane had her last chemo, whenever that would be.

Ten days after Jane's fourth treatment things were going pretty well for her, and I continued to interview combat veterans for my book. She was just getting sick and tired of feeling sick and tired, and I was getting sick and tired of seeing her feeling sick and tired. But we knew better days were ahead of us. If all went well, she would be through with her radiation before we left for Ft. Myers at the end of December. It did and we did.

In the meantime, the cards and notes kept pouring in from friends, relatives and our church family. It was distressing, however, not hearing from a few friends with whom we had been close with over the years. It was like we had a plague that could be caught over the telephone wires or by sending a card. That taught us how important it is to keep in touch when others are in similar situations.

The day after Michigan elected its first female governor, November 6, 2002, we heard the words that sent both of us nearly to tears. Dr. Hurtebise approved giving Jane only four chemo treatments instead of the earlier prescribed six, and the following day she had a consultation with the radiologist

On Wednesday, November 13 Jane had her first treatment of radiation and three more that week. Thirty more to go.

The radiation was successful and we left for our winter home on schedule.

On the family front in 2002, our Christmas letter read, in part: *Brenda's family continues living near Battle Creek, where all the kids are involved in school activities. Jodi (13) struts her stuff as a cheerleader for the Jr. Varsity athletic teams and Kevin (16) is building a job resume as a cook at a nearby Subway eatery while making good grades in school. Jennifer (10) is busy raising a miniature hamster.*

Dave is enjoying his job as Midland County's 4-H director and will be enjoying a trip to Japan as part of the program next year. His oldest daughter, Stacy, now a 17-year-old, is wowing audiences in Clare as a Thespian in her Drama Club, and Ashley, 15, is a member of the Clare High School Band, and is wowing her grandparents as a saxophonist in a jazz band.

CHAPTER TWELVE

Life is like a sailing ship—when the seas become rough
and stormy you need to adjust your sails.
—Elizabeth Edwards

2002 continued to be a year of frustration as we lost a wonderful family man in our family. Brother-in-law, Gene, sister Bernadine's husband succumbed to cancer.

It was a tearful funeral, as most are. But Bernie and her family being Catholic, made it less tearful for us Protestants. We didn't know what was going on most of the time during the service. Catholic ceremonies are so staid and by the book. The whole thing became mechanical, with seemingly very little compassion. The priest's voice sounded like he did that sort of thing a dozen times a week and this was just another one. But guess it's what one becomes accustomed to.

At one point the priest asked that we take a moment of silence and think about what the deceased meant to us. Crap, let's stand up and TELL everyone what the deceased meant to us! I was ready to, but was not asked to do so. The family would have liked to hear that. But maybe only if one is Protestant. Just as well. I'm certain I would have choked anyway and embarrassed the whole family.

The impressive part came after the service. Gene had been a voluntary fireman in Lake Odessa for thirty years. Fire departments from the surrounding communities, plus the local one, formed an honor guard from the church. The pall bearers carried the casket through the guard and placed it on an antique fire truck. That, and the other fire-fighting vehicles, led the parade to the cemetery. As the casket passed through the guard, they stood at attention and saluted. I couldn't help but give him a snappy salute myself as the casket passed by. Gene was really a neat guy, and I loved him like a brother.

CHAPTER THIRTEEN

Good friends are like stars . . . you don't always see them
but you know they are always there.

The year 2003 ended much better than it began. By the end of January Jane's hair had grown back to the point where she no longer needed her wig or baseball cap. She loved the new curly and wavy hair, and we spent a wonderful winter at our new winter home in Ft. Myers. In March the winter was topped off with a ten-day cruise to the West Indies, visiting the islands of St. Martin, St. Kitts, St. Lucia, St. Thomas (no relation) and Barbados. Our good friends, Dave and Jan Weissenborn were also with us, as were some others from our winter home at Plantation Estates.

In September that year we had one of the most beautiful trips in our lives. With our traveling companions, Dave and Jan, we did the Canadian Rockies. We flew from Detroit to Calgary. Much of the trip was by tour bus, but the final two days were on a domed train from Alberta, Vancouver and all points in between. It was wonderful!

Added to the fun, were the attendants on the trip. As on our cruise to the West Indies, Dave and I chided each other about how much the female attendants patronized us. During dinner, the discussion might go, "Dave, did you notice how she gave me the eye and barely looked at you?" Or, "Lowell, did you notice she served me before you? I'm certain she likes me best."

At the end of each trip, the beautiful attendant, sometimes of Philippine or Scandinavian descent, would come up to me in front of Dave and give me a big hug and would tell me how much she would miss me.

I would then turn and give a wink to Dave, who just stood there wondering where that came from. What he didn't know was that "where that came from" was the five dollar bill I would slip each one to do that after I had explained, on the side, why I wanted her to do that. I would have paid twice that much just to have those beauties hug me.

Anyway, Dave was such a good sport about it, and a good friend, that I later told him how that all came about. We both had hearty chuckles and he had to comment, "At least when I get hugged I don't have to pay for it." He might have been right, but I never saw him get hugged either.

The manuscript for my book, *Silent Heroes,* went to the publisher at Michigan State University Press in December, knowing it could be at least a year before it appeared in book stores in Midland.

CHAPTER FOURTEEN

A writer is someone for whom writing
is more difficult than it is for other people.
— *Thomas Mann, Novelist*

If, after plodding through 2003 and one found it even a little exciting, 2004 was off the charts.

Michiko and Yoshi were back; Michiko for the second time. They attended a friend's wedding in Big Rapids and their four days with us were much too short. While I love Yoshi and his smile like a brother, I still would like to have adopted Michiko. They were so much fun to have around. And Yoshi had learned a little more English.

2004 offered big changes for Kevin and Stacy. Kevin began his freshman year in architecture at Lawrence Tech University in Southfield and Stacy became a freshman at Hope College in Holland, MI as a drama major. Her "hamminess" fit the Hope curriculum perfectly.

The previous November my book went to press and this year we went through several editings and proof readings for the next several months. Originally, the Midland County Historical (I later dubbed it the Hysterical) Society was going to sponsor it, pay for it, promote it and pay me a $10,000 fee for writing it. They would then own the copyright. Fine with me.

But it didn't turn out that way. The Society didn't keep promise one, including the legal document, which they had asked me to write. I submitted it twice without the slightest response. The director of the Society never returned my phone calls and paid little attention to e-mails.

After two years of this nonsense (all this time I was interviewing and writing), Jane and I decided that we would pay the $14,000 publishing bill and hope we came out even. (We eventually made just over $6,000).

That was fine with us too. We got to keep the copyright, and the veterans received the attention they had long deserved.

The book release had been set and highly publicized for November 11, 2004 (Veteran's Day) at the Grace A. Dow Library in Midland. Working with the library for several weeks, they would provide space in their auditorium for my presentation of the book and provide refreshments afterward. They were the most cordial hosts one would want.

But like the landing on Omaha Beach during World War II, it was not without its pitfalls. Only this time it was anxiety that nearly took us down.

The semi-trailer that delivered the 1,000 books to our house had to back down our curving dirt road in the woods on Wixom Lake because there was no place for a rig that size to turn around. They were delivered on November 2, 2004, just ten days before the general election which elected George W. Bush to his second term of office (which has absolutely nothing to do with this chapter).

Anyway, it wasn't until the following morning that I realized a major mistake in the printing had occurred. I rose early as usual, around 6:00 a.m. and began admiring the work of my Pulitzer Prize winner. To my horror, I soon discovered that the first two pages of the table of Contents did not match the page numbers of the text.

In near panic, I called Michigan State University Press promptly at 8:00 a.m. Release date was only ten days away. I had learned from experience over the past year, however, that no one at the Press ever answered their telephone. It goes promptly into voice mail. Often that never got a response, or it might take two or three days for a reply. E-mail was normally the way to go.

Either it was my E-mail or the frustration in my voice, but a phone call was returned within fifteen minutes from my contact to the Press.

The response was, "We will have them picked up tomorrow (this was a Thursday), and have 300 copies corrected and returned to you next week. "Sorry," I blurted out, "That is not acceptable. This book has been highly publicized in the Midland Community, and we will sell more than that during the book launch at the library."

"We will do the best we can," the voice said non-committally.

The next day the semi-trailer backed its way once again to our driveway to pick up the books. When it arrived, I asked the driver, "Do you take these directly to the printer in Ann Arbor?" His reply was, "No, I take these to Saginaw where they will be loaded onto a truck for Toledo. Toledo serves the Ann Arbor area." Good grief!! (Even though the MSU Press was in East Lansing, the books were actually printed in Ann Arbor).

For the third time, the 18-wheeler backed its way through the woods, down the half-mile of winding road to our driveway, but with all 1,000 copies corrected, just thirty-six hours from launch time. Someone got overtime pay all weekend at the printing company in Ann Arbor. And Jane and I got a wonderful sigh of relief!

What a terrific experience. The people at the Grace A. Dow Library did a marvelous job of hosting the book launch with smiles, refreshments and publicity posters they had designed and printed and posted throughout the library.

I had asked old friends, Don and Marjorie Abbott to be with us. We had known them since our college days, when we first met. Don was a retired jet pilot from the Vietnam era and both he and Marge had stood with us at our wedding in 1958. Don was also one of the endorsers on the back cover my book.

In it he had written,

> *As a military pilot of twenty-six years, I know it is difficult to get military veterans to relate their combat experiences. The experiences of those in this book are a vital part of the history of Midland County . . . they are real, gripping and sometimes unpleasant. This should be mandatory reading for all high school history students."—Lt. Col. Donald L. Abbott (Ret.), United States Air Force Vietnam Veteran.*

Also in the audience of approximately 200, were Jane (of course), Brenda, Kevin (who had skipped a day of his freshman year at Lawrence Tech), Jodi (who skipped a day of her freshman year at Gull Lake High School) Ashley, whose school was out that day anyway and friends, Doug and Sandie Butler. It should be noted that the *Midland Daily News* and its marketing director, Kevin Prior, a friend of mine, gave me countless columns and advertisements leading toward that day and the days that followed. I was never charged for the ads. In fact, the *Midland Daily News* offered to sell the book from their counter in the front lobby. By Christmas we had sold approximately 700 copies.

On stage with me were a couple WWII veterans whose stories were in the book. In addition, was Terry Moore, whom I had asked to introduce me. Terry and I went back a long way. He was the CEO for the Midland Hospital Center and a noted author of books on hospital administration. He was also a noted speaker who helped me out with a program when I was president of the Saginaw Valley Chapter of the American Society for Training and Development (ASTD). That was in the early 1990s and we had been friends ever since. As always, Terry did a masterful job and gave me more accolades than I probably deserved. Terry's gracious endorsement also appears on the back cover. It reads,

> *Lowell Thomas has not forgotten the people among us who sacrificed so much and witnessed things most of us will never see. Mr. Thomas has broken the silence of those heroes and in so doing has preserved a piece of history that is a worthwhile read for people of all ages. I couldn't put it down. I recommend it highly.*

While I was introducing the book, I mentioned that one of the subjects was a veteran of the Bolshevik Revolution in 1918. And it was the first story in the book. I mentioned that few people living today had ever heard of it, but that the Americans were very much involved in it. President Woodrow Wilson was then the Commander-in-Chief who once stated that the Americans would never become involved in the war with the Russians in the Arctic Circle. He changed his mind.

I interviewed the kindly gentleman from the Bolshevik Revolution, Oscar Holstrom, wrote his story and it appeared in the *Midland Daily News* on September 20, 1983. It was his 89th birthday. What a delightful gentleman was he.

Anyway, as I mentioned the story, and how few living people today had ever heard of the Revolution, a pretty white-haired lady in the auditorium raised her hand and said, "I've heard of it." Asking her about it, she said, "Oscar Holstrom was my father." I was so delighted, and stunned, that the only thing I could think of doing was to ask the audience to give her applause. I might have even choked up.

Just over 300 copies were sold and autographed on that brisk November 11, 2004, with the line of people winding around from the stage to the back of the auditorium. Some friends left at that point, knowing they could get a copy later and not have to stand in line. Jane, Brenda, Jodi, and Ashley were all involved with selling or "crowd control" and Kevin, dressed like he was going to a job interview, stood beside me and turned the page in each book to where I would sign it, and handed it to me. It saved a great deal of time for those waiting in line.

CHAPTER FIFTEEN

Fifteen minutes of fame is probably enough for most people.
Any more and it could make for an undesirable person.

It's a thrilling experience, writing a book, having your friends endorse it, and having hundreds standing in line to purchase one, but this current Volume of my autobiography, like its predecessor (*So Far . . . So Good . . .*), will be given away to family and close friends. I don't mind. I don't even mind if some of my friends and family take time to read it.

I further didn't mind having an old friend and former employee in adult education, Jan Marcou, ask me to record the book *Silent Heroes* and have it distributed to the sight-impaired in Midland and Gladwin Counties. Jan was then working for the Midland/Gladwin Chapter of the American Red Cross. I began recording it, and was not terribly pleased. Lacking high-tech equipment, I turned it over to someone at the Red Cross office (a volunteer) who was supposedly adept at such performances. I listened to some of his tapes and not overly impressed with those either. He lacked the "feeling" for war stories, in my judgment, but I was perhaps too close to be subject. I don't know if the audios were ever distributed. Jan had left her Red Cross position by this time and the director had passed on. I never asked the new people the outcome.

Promoting the book was the fun part . . . much like promoting adult and continuing education during my career days. While the *Midland Daily News* was most helpful, as was WMPX radio station, I tried to think outside the box.

One "outside the box" idea put me in touch, at least through automated e-mail, with the legendary Oprah Winfrey. I learned her e-mail address and wrote her about my book and that it was a take-off on Tom Brokaw's best-seller, *The Greatest Generation*. I didn't mind dropping the name of someone she probably knew personally.

The answer came back by e-mail, saying:
From: Oprah.com <Oprah.com@oprah.com>
Subject: Oprah.com has received your e-mail
To: ltandjt@yahoo.com
Date: Thursday, September 9, 2004, 3:31 AM

Dear Lowell Thomas,

Thank you for your e-mail! Your message is important to us. Unfortunately, due to the volume of e-mail messages we receive every day, we cannot guarantee that you'll receive a personal response. Feel free to check out our Frequently Asked Questions for additional help. http://www.oprah.com/tows/program/tows_prog_main.jhtml

Thanks again for writing to us!

Sincerely,
The Oprah.com Staff
www.oprah.com

At least I received a reply, and from her whole staff yet. Yeah right!

But it was an exciting time for Jane and me. I contacted many people in the Midland area I had known from previous years and I knew to which groups and clubs they belonged. Between October and December of 2004, I spoke to 22 different groups such as the Rotary Clubs, Lion Clubs, women's groups, men's groups and many others. In many situations some of the men in the book were in these groups. When I knew they were, I would read several paragraphs of their story, and then asked the group if they knew whom I was talking about. I would present, to the first one to give the correct answer, a ball point pen with the name of the book on it. It was a fun game and with the exception of a couple groups, I would sell anywhere from one to a dozen copies of the book.

One February day, while we were in our winter home in Ft. Myers, I received a telephone call from a lady at the Barnes and Noble Booksellers in Midland. (Our Florida telephone number was given out by our answering machine at home).

She asked if I would be willing to do a book signing at their store. Trying to hide my excitement, I said that I would but that it would have to wait until May when we arrived home from Florida. It was agreed. The date was set.

When we arrived home three months later, I stopped in at Barnes and Noble to meet this wonderful lady and to see my own book on the shelves of this prestigious book store.

I discovered they might be Barnes, but they were not very noble. They had the book outrageously overpriced. I was selling this Pulitzer Prize for $29, including tax, as was the *Midland Daily News* and Mesler's Men's Store in Midland. The Midland Center for the Arts was selling it for $29 plus tax (I sold them a box of thirty-six for $23). Glover's Pharmacy sold 100 of them for $34 (I sold them to Glover's for $23) plus tax, as was a book store in Gladwin. And I had autographed each one of them. Barnes and Noble was asking $39 plus tax, making the total $41.34. For some reason they couldn't purchase them directly from me, but I knew what they had paid for them through their agents to the publisher. They were making more money on each book than I was, and I had done all the work.

I cancelled the book signing, informing them that the public could buy one of the books for over $12 less at several locations in town. Barnes and Nobel was not a happy camper. They had already put out publicity (along with a lot of other irrelevant information). Frankly, I didn't care. Highway robbery by any other name is still highway robbery.

I also knew, by reading writer's literature, that if an author sells four or five books at a two-hour book signing, he/she is very fortunate. I wasn't about to waste my time to help make Barnes and Nobel wealthy by enticing the public into their store to make other purchases.

I was criticized by fellow authors for my actions, but I was the one who still had to live with myself. I had already had my fifteen minutes of fame and that's more than many people have in a lifetime.

By the time we had left Florida for home, we had already sold 36 books to friends and friends of friends in Ft. Myers.

My satisfaction, however, came more from the accolades of relatives and friends of the veterans in the stories. All had been published in the *Midland Daily News* over the years, prior to their being published in my book. And, since my e-mail address and phone number followed each story in the paper, most of the responses were by e-mail.

One note I received on August 20, 2002 read:

I just read your article "Local Veteran Will Never Forget His 21ˢᵗ Birthday" of my Uncle Don Harrington. I just started to learn about some of his World War II encounters when he wrote about his experiences. Maybe you were the one to bring them to paper?

Thanks, I will be keeping a copy with the "Family Tree" information for my boys.

Gene Harrington
Akron, Michigan

On November 24, 2002, the following note, in part, came from a relative of one of the veterans I had interviewed.

Hello Lowell,

Thank you so much for sending the story to me. I know you have made several trips to see Woody to get the story. He did enjoy those visits and I am sure is very proud of the story.

You have a most interesting job doing these first-hand interviews and recording other people's stories. Thank you again for recognizing Woody and your correspondence with me.

Sincerely,
Diane Heppner

(I believe Diane was a niece who lived out of state. She didn't give her return address).

Yet another, in part, is a response from a close friend of a World War II and Korean Conflict veteran in the book:

Lowell:

I am so glad that you found Lyle (Eastman) *and made him a subject for your* (newspaper) *piece . . . . you caught his unassuming approach to his wartime experiences. With all due respect, he is typical of the "grunts"*

57

who actually fight our wars without expecting recognition of any sort and only try to survive.

I am so glad our government recently awarded him a belated Korean War Medal which he had earned and had been approved in 1953.

Maybe I am writing this on the eve of an election because we have endured unending shameless self-promotion from political leaders who wrap themselves in the flag and "have other priorities" when the dirty work has to be done by the Lyle Eastman's.

Len Battle
Midland

I appreciated Len's comments because I had met him many years before and had the deepest respect for him. He was also an appreciated and respected attorney in the community for many years.

Kevin Renwick, a World War II combat veteran, had a friend of the highest rank who wrote me saying:

Hello Mr. Thomas

I read your article on Roy Renwick and found it very interesting. Kevin Renwick passed the article to me a few months ago when I was back home in Midland. I did not read it at the time and just today pulled it out of the things to do, and realized Roy must be Kevin's father or uncle.

If you have other articles on Midland residents I would sure like to read them.

Rear Admiral Vernon C. Smith, USN Ret.
Virginia Beach, VA

(I don't remember if I sent him any other stories from my book).

Another kind note was e-mailed to me from a lady in Traverse City on January 23, 2003 and read, in part:

Mr. Thomas,

Thank you for publishing the article regarding Bill Elliott in the Midland Daily News. My neighbor, Shirley Brasie, also originally from Midland, shared the article with me. I have known Bill (Elliot) since back in the 60's . . . .

Bill is a remarkable person, whom I greatly admire and respect.

Sincerely,
Kay Schmaizried
Traverse City, MI

(Bill was a World War II veteran).

Some of the e-mail letters I received nearly brought tears. One of them was from the niece of one of my subjects. It went like this and it was dated, April 6, 2003:

Dear Mr. Thomas,

My name is Kimberly Foote, my uncle is Bob Mesler whom you wrote the wonderful story, "A Positive Attitude Saved His Life." What a wonderful job you did!!

I can remember as a little girl seeing a very special scrap book that my Grandma Mesler kept containing old letters and postcards from my Uncle Bob. I did not understand that he was a "prisoner of war." As I got older I would ask my father about Uncle Bob being a prisoner of war. He would tell me a few things that he remembered about being a young boy with a brother that was a POW. It seemed a topic that was best not brought up.

I have not been fortunate enough to hear him speak on this topic. He is my "God Father" and next to my Dad has always been very special and somewhat of a hero. I can now say, with your help, he is a true hero to me. Thank you!

I would very much like to purchase your book. I am not in the Midland area. I have tried looking up the Midland Historical Society but I have been unsuccessful. Could you please help me? I would like to get 3 copies. One for myself, my father and my brother. This will truly be a family keepsake brought to us BY YOU!

Kimberly Foote

Harrison, MI

(I e-mailed Kim and told her the nearest place to purchase the books was in Gladwin, and gave her the name of the store. It would be about a 15 minute drive for her. Later I learned from her that she had made the purchase).

Probably the most moving e-mail letter I received was from Sharon Troyer from Colorado. Her father was a World War II hero whose job was to diffuse or detonate bombs in areas where the U.S. and its allies bombed but had not exploded upon contact with the earth.

Her letter, in its entirety, and dated May 15, 2003, went like this:

Dear Lowell,

I've been meaning to send you a thank you for the article you did on my Dad, Robert Graves, which was in the March 9 Midland Daily News. Many people called him after seeing it.

I saw an initial draft of your interview with him when I was home and I can't tell you how proud I was when I received the actual newspaper copy. My Dad felt proud to tell his story and your work was a great tribute to the sacrifices he made in WWII. He said it felt good to be able to talk about it after all these years. He really trusted you with the volumes of information that came out during the interview.

Over the last few years, he began sharing some of his experiences during the war with me, but I learned something new about my Dad from the article. I never understood why he was a "loner" and he explained it as not trusting anyone but himself in order to make it back home. I know him better now.

Part of my reason for writing to you is that he turns 80 years old on Monday, May 19. My dream of him someday having his stories in print has come true. Thanks again.

Sincerely,
Sharon Troyer

(I called Bob on his 80th birthday and he was tremendously appreciative. Sharon and I corresponded numerous times after that and she shared the same traits as her father).

One of the most complimentary notes came from my editor, Barbara Prince Sovereen. I had known Barb briefly and her husband, Lovell, was one the subjects in the book. He was on Iwo Jima when the American flag was raised on Mt. Suribachi. I knew that she had once worked in public relations for the Dow Corning Corporation in Midland and had done a lot of writing, both for them and for the *Midland Daily News.* She had even edited a story I had done for the MDN and asked it to be sent to Corning to be placed in their PR publication. It was about a retiree from the company who had begun his own company. I didn't get a byline for it, but did receive a check for $75, the most I had ever received (at the time) for something I had written.

Anyway, Barb sent a handwritten note, when returning some of her editing, stating:

> *I'll bet you sell a million of these (Silent Heroes). I know of at least five (and maybe more for the grandchildren) in our house.*
> *Good luck. This is a wonderful idea.*
>
> > *Barb*
> > *10-12-02*

Bless her heart! I never did sell her predicted million copies, but I was happy with the 1200 I did sell. I know that some ended up as far away as California, Australia, Europe and Japan.

Before I leave the saga of *Silent Heroes,* I should mention four other friends who endorsed the book.

One was Jim Clark, a former principal of a high school in Midland who had been elevated to director of curriculum for the Midland Public Schools prior to his retirement. Jim relates,

> *The stories in Silent Heroes are about survivors. These Midland County veterans tell of their real battle experiences during wartime. You realize "war is hell" and not as glorified as Hollywood filmmakers often depict. Combat veterans are now telling of the ravages of war and giving us history lessons not found in textbooks.*

Dorothy Langdon Yates, author of five books on the history of Midland wrote:

> *This is war like it is. Lowell Thomas's heroes have broken their silence to tell their grim stories. A gripping read.*

Still another, Stephen Tracy, a Vietnam Veteran whose story is included in the book, and was, at the time, the veteran's counselor for Midland County wrote,

> *You feel the excitement, along with the discomforts and pleasures unique to military life. This book details the war experiences of Midland County's combat veterans in places and situations unique to war veterans.*

I am extremely proud to have known those who endorsed my book because I had respected all of them for many, many years with my professional and personal contacts.

My most recent contact, however, and is explained in another chapter, is Colonel Robert K. Morgan (Ret.). Colonel Morgan was the pilot of the famed B-17, named the *Memphis Belle*. Morgan was the first pilot to fly his crew twenty-five missions over Europe in World War II without a casualty. I wasn't even in my teens when this happened, but I remember hearing the name of his infamous airplane. He later headed the first B-29 raid over Tokyo.

Sending him an unedited manuscript in 2003, asking for an endorsement, he wrote back, saying,

> *Lowell Thomas has put together an excellent group of stories about military persons from Midland County in combat, expressed candidly and with personal feeling. An excellent read.*

I was delighted beyond belief. Unfortunately, the Colonel died from an injury in falling. Ironically, it happened at an airport and was unrelated to flying.

While working for the most of three years (actually, some of the veteran's stories I had written twenty years before for the *Midland Daily News*. (Fortunately I had saved them). During the final years of writing

I became very familiar with the subjects and when I knew their birth date, sent them a birthday card. Often when the telephone rang and Jane answered it, she would turn to me and say, "It's one of your boys." The "boys" were all in their 80's, thanking me for my thoughtfulness.

Before I leave the subject of the book, I must add a bit of humor as a response from one of my book purchasers. She had retired as a nurse in a local hospital in Ft. Myers, but wasn't terribly tactful. While showing the book to friends in our mobile home park in Florida in 2004, this lady, obviously an educated one, said, "I'd like to buy one of your books, Lowell. I'll probably never read it, but I've never known an author before." Nothing like honesty with a sense of humor. Except she was serious. She bought the book.

CHAPTER SIXTEEN

Be careful what you write. Someone just might read it.

Silent Heroes was the seventh book I had either authored or co-authored, but the only one that had been sold on the open market. The others were either for personal pleasure or for a specific business. They are listed here in order and by date published:

1970—*A Tree Grows in Midland*
1980—*The Tree Still Grows in Midland*
> The above describes the growth of the adult education program in the Midland Public Schools since its inception in 1923. Twenty of those years I was its director.

1981—*Sales and Customer Service: Retailing*
> This book was co-authored with Dan Andrews, owner of Andrews Consulting in Saginaw. It was sold to several Michigan adult education programs and to the Meijer's food store chain for in-service training when they opened their doors in Midland.

1985—*Sales Promotion in Adult Education*
> This was written as a presentation to public school and university adult education directors, extension directors and anyone involved in continuing education in any form of professional continuing education when I was doing nation-wide programs for the Bureau of Education and Technology out of New York City.

1990—*Grandpa's Stories*
> After taking a correspondence course from a school in Connecticut, these stories were edited, bound and given as Christmas presents to Brenda, Dave and our five grandchildren.

2000—*So Far . . . So Good: The Other Lowell Thomas Story*
 Volume I of my autobiography, given to Brenda, Dave and their
 families for Christmas that year.
2004—*Silent Heroes*
 Enough has been said about this one.
2005—*Silent Heroes of Plantation Estates*
 This was an off-shoot of the Midland County *Silent Heroes* and
 depicts the "silent heroes" of combat veterans in our mobile home
 park in Ft. Myers, FL. It also includes the stories of three people
 who grew up in Hitler's Germany.

A few of my publications

CHAPTER SEVENTEEN

No rules are made for the minority.

After over two years of writing, proof-reading and editing, the final manuscript of *Silent Heroes* was sent to the publisher's for the last time there was a great let-down. Also a great relief! With abundant time on our hands, Jane and I decided there was nothing more we could do to improve nor hasten the publication of *Silent Heroes*.

We have always been prone to adventure, so we headed for one of our favorite places on earth . . . Maine and the Northeast Coast. Of course, one of our favorite reasons was that in the several times we had visited there, there was an abundance of lobster at realistic prices. And we looovve lobster!

On September 26, 2004 we left for lobster land bright and early (6:00 a.m.). As it turned out, it was early, but we weren't too bright. In our haste, there were a number of things we wished we had taken . . . like the electric cord to the cooler . . . and forgetting to call AAA for maps. (This was before a GPS ever arrived on the scene).

Fortunately, we found motels along the way with refrigerators so we could take things from the cooler (which was in the trunk, which connected to the cigarette lighter inside the car). And Jane did fairly well navigating using an old Atlas we had in the car.

We drove just over 600 miles the first day and just over 300 the second, arriving on the East Coast about 3:30 p.m on the 27th. But that included lunch in Lowell, Massachusetts.

Not so ironically, I found a sweatshirt, coffee mug and a baseball cap with my name on them. It didn't even say "Massachusetts" on them. But the real attraction for me was a T-shirt with the city's logo on it that read, "There's something to like about Lowell." I have used them all often, gathering smiles and wise cracks from friends.

66

And that's interesting too. When I was growing up, people of my generation, when I was introduced to them would ask, "Are you related to the other Lowell Thomas?" The "other" Lowell Thomas was a world renown news broadcaster and author of 52 books (I have seven of his books he personally autographed for me). Whenever Jane and I were in a strange city and made a restaurant reservation, we always had the best seat in the house . . . that even included Hawaii during the 1970's. Hey, if they don't ask, don't tell. The "other" Lowell Thomas was also the first newsman to broadcast the news from a war zone in World War II. The interesting part is that the generations that followed, whenever I make a hotel or restaurant reservation and give them my name, I am frequently asked, "How do you spell that?"

Anyway, that's how the first volume of my autobiography came to be called, *So Far . . . So Good; The Other Lowell Thomas Story.*

But back to <u>this</u> story. We so much liked the area and its old houses and Inns and the Atlantic beaches of Maine. Many of the stores, having made their millions from the tourists during the summer, had already closed for the season. They seemed somewhat like ghost towns except for the few working red lights. Which we caught with abandon.

We had a wonderful lobster dinner at the Cascades that first night. Two complete lobsters for only $17.95, along with baked potato and salad. It was right up there with a good orgasm. Heavenly!!

The next day we had lunch with an old Army buddy, Dr. Clifford Thompson, from Portland (three degrees from Harvard and who taught at Harvard for a few years). In keeping with our mission for going to Maine, Jane had a lobster sandwich and I had lobster stew.

For the first time, Cliff admitted that maybe he had missed something by not getting married and having kids and grandkids. (It takes a Ph.D. from Harvard to figure that out?).

It was good seeing Cliff again, who had been in our home a couple times over the years. But it had been at least five years since we had last seen him. Cliff never had a computer so we always kept in touch by phone or U.S. mail.

That evening we went back to the same restaurant as the night before and once more loaded up on lobster. And more Heaven! OK, it wasn't all heaven, and I was the cause. As we were seated in the large restaurant area, we noticed a lady, OK, maybe not a lady, but at least a woman seated at the next table with a cell phone growing out of her left ear. Her right hand was shoveling in her lobster like it was the last one in the house and she had to protect it.

Jane said, "Let's ask for a different table." About that time the waiter appeared at our side, and in a voice loud enough to be heard half-way to the parking lot I said, "If that lady is going to talk on her cell phone all night, we'd like another table." He assured us we could have any table in the room. The restaurant was only about a quarter full (you know how "early birds" are) so we picked out a cozy little spot in the corner next to a window and out of earshot of the one-sided conversation.

The sad part was that there were signs in the entryway to the eating area, stating that cell phones were prohibited. The night before, I had even thanked the maitre'd for having the signs up. Obviously, they meant nothing.

That evening we took a stroll along the beach. The ocean swells were illuminated under a full moon. Almost surreal. And beautiful!

The next day we decided to head south for Kennebunkport (about 15 miles), perhaps spend the night and start home the following day. It wasn't that simple. Jane began reading literature of the immediate area and realized she had missed a large mall a few miles north of us.

So, of course, we took the scenic route, getting to Kennebunkport about noon, just in time for lunch. How very fortunate. Fortunate too, that we were directed to the best lobster diner in the area. Not very big, but the palate had a real treat. We split a three-pound platter of lobster (already plucked from the shell), plus the usual salad, etc. Along with a half-carafe of White Zin, plus a generous tip, the tab came to $78 . . . and worth every cent. It was a great way to conclude four meals in three days of lobster-gorging.

Following lunch, we drove down the coast to view the first George's (Bush) summer home. Not terribly impressive from the distance we viewed it, but I did zoom in to get a picture with the digital camera.

At one point, thanks to the lack of AAA maps, we realized we were lost (which was becoming a habit), so we stopped to ask a pretty young thing strolling on the grass-lined sidewalk, for directions. While she seemed to know what she was talking about, she must have just been off the boat from jolly old London Town. Her English accent was so strong it wouldn't have even made good tea. When we parted ways I asked Jane what the hell the lady had said. Says Jane, "I haven't a clue." We just kept emptying the tank until we found our own way.

Anyway, before we left the motel that morning, Jane called our credit card company to learn that her last check had arrived, thus giving her a clean slate on which to work.

That night we stayed in Worcester, Massachusetts, at a nice Best Western. Nice, large room, plus a nice pool and exercise room. Never did we use the latter two, but nice to know they were there if we had wanted to. It was also nice to be able to use the laptop on their internet service. That was good because I needed to reply to a note from Michigan State University, who was publishing my book, *Silent Heroes.*

We didn't rush away Thursday morning. We had a good "free" hot and cold breakfast at the motel and pulled out about 9:00 a.m. After about four hours we stopped off for lunch and shuffled off toward Buffalo (NY), finding a motel called Microtel. It gave new meaning to the word "micro." Only our linen closet at home is smaller. But it was nearly 6:00 p.m. and we were stressed out from the day. The hotel also advertised "free" internet service .They just didn't say it didn't work . . . which it didn't!

Our education also continued when we found that in New England they drive at only three speeds . . . fast, faster and go like hell! We seldom found a cop on the highway and concluded that only fools feared to tread there.

We got lost only a couple times in Canada between Buffalo and Port Huron (MI).

After we finally got back into the U.S. of A., where we no longer had to compute kilometers into miles, we headed north toward Flint and an hour layover at brother Doug's. It was good to see them again. Hadn't seen them since summer, the previous year. We arrived home about 3:30 and it was good to crawl into our own bed again that night.

That was just one of our trips to the East Coast in the fall of the year, but will save the reader the boredom of plowing (or skipping altogether) through them. Just know that New England in the fall is much like Michigan . . . beautiful!

CHAPTER EIGHTEEN

Life is not about waiting for the storms to pass . . .
it's about learning how to dance in the rain.

It was a crisp, bright day on November 11, 2004, when over 200 people gathered in the Little Theater at the Grace A. Dow Library in Midland to join in the launching of *Silent Heroes*. Below is a portion of my welcoming speech to the crowd, which tells of how we got to that day. Terry Moore, CEO of Midland Hospital, a long-time friend and author of several books on hospital administration, introduced me.

Thank you Terry, and welcome all to Veteran's Day, 2004. A day when we honor those who have fought for those freedoms we still believe in and have helped keep us safe from those who are hell-bent on destroying us.

When I first picked up the book, I couldn't help but notice from the pictures, what good looking, debonair, clean-cut young men who were sent off to war. I have just one question—what happened? (A lot of laughs).

And welcome to the launching of <u>Silent Heroes</u>. Many months ago, Virginia McKane, here at the library, contacted me to see if we would be willing to hold the unveiling of this book right here and the library would provide refreshments.

I was honored, but I said, "Let's call it a 'Book Launching.'" After all, launching is a military term. I thought that "unveiling" was a term the new groom does to the bride just before he kisses her at the alter.

This "launching," is somewhat like the launching of troops on Iwo Jima in World War II, or the launching of the bombing raids over Tokyo, or the launching of wounded troops out of the frozen snow of Korea or the launching of troops into the steaming jungles of Vietnam. This launching had its pitfalls too.

More than once, we bit the bullet and moved on. When I say "we," I am including my wife, Jane in this because she has been right there in the trenches with me to see this through. When this project began, we sought financing through various sources. When we could see that wasn't going to happen in time, we said, "We can do this ourselves!" We were so determined that these stories should be out there.

And you know what? It was easy. It was no different than buying a new car . . . but then selling it quick before it depreciates!

A year ago this month, University Press at MSU called me to say they would publish the book. December 1 of last year I submitted the final manuscript. It wasn't until four months later, in April this year, that I received the production schedule.

The schedule said we would have the first proof draft by June 19. But I went to the bottom line and said the book HAD to be ready by November 1. (I later learned that you don't tell a publisher what they HAVE to do). *The proof didn't arrive until the first of August and I wondered right away what that would do to the date on the bottom line.*

The bottom line remained the same . . . until we began planning in earnest for the launch. We were told that it would be a couple weeks later than November 1. I looked at the calendar and discovered that November 11 is Veteran's Day. What could be more appropriate? So we set today as the launch date and informed the publisher. Just so they wouldn't forget, I also informed them of the library's cooperation, the posters and flyers they had made and distributed around town, and the work the Midland Daily News had done to get the word out again and again and again.

Bless their hearts, the books arrived by UPS at my garage last week Monday, November 1 . . . all 1,000 copies of them. They were shipped back to the printer's in Ann Arbor the following day . . . Election Day! (George W. Bush won). *Early the next morning, I discovered that half the page numbers in the Table of Contents were wrong. It said, for example, that Bob Mesler's story was on page 175, when in fact, it might have been on page 142. The first two pages of the Contents were wrong, even though I had told them they were wrong during the final proof reading.*

Now, you have to understand something about the publishing business. They <u>never</u> answer the telephone. Your message <u>always</u> goes to voice mail, and they call you back at <u>their</u> convenience . . . a few days later. But my experience had told me they checked their E-mail several times each day.

We were ten days from launch and I wasn't very kind. Ten minutes later the phone rang. It was the Printer's mistake, according to the publisher, but was fixable. It would take something we didn't have much of . . . time. The bottom line was that the printer, in Ann Arbor, would send a truck to pick up the books by 5:00 p.m. that day. That was last week Tuesday, nine days before launch date.

When they said "truck," they meant TRUCK! It was an 18-wheeler! The few of you who have been to our home know that the last 4/10 of a mile is off the main road, on a little dirt road back in the woods on Wixom Lake. You also know there are two sharp curves in that 4/10 of a mile. The 18-wheeler had to back his rig down that 4/10 of a mile and maneuver around the curves because we are also on a dead end road and there is no room for an 18-wheeler to turn around.

As I helped the driver load the 28 boxes of books onto his truck, I asked if he would be taking the books right to Ann Arbor. He replied that he would take them to the terminal in Saginaw where they would be loaded onto another truck for Toledo, then loaded onto another truck for Ann Arbor. That was NOT pleasant news.

On Friday of last week I received an e-mail from the publisher stating that at least 300 corrected copies would be shipped on Tuesday the 9th. Delivery date was two days ago. Even though I had kept the publisher aware of all the promotion going on these past few weeks, I reminded them that there could be nearly that many people here today, plus this Saturday, the 13th, from 9 a.m. to 4 p.m., we will be at the all-day arts and crafts fair at Assumption Catholic Church . . . one of the largest such activities in the area. And from 5 p.m. until 7 p.m. Saturday evening, we will be at a book signing at the Sanford American Legion's Annual Dinner, and not that everyone there will want a book, they do expect 150 in attendance. (Plus, I intended to give a book to each of those who helped me by endorsing it on the back cover, my kids and grandkids and five copies to the Grace A. Dow Library for all they had done for me).

Long story short . . . (I then summed up how the books arrived thirty-six hours prior to launch).

I have to tell you that I proofed each of these stories at least four times before they ever went to the Midland Daily News. I proofed them three more times for the publisher. Barb Sovereen, bless her heart, proofed them twice,

then insisted she look at them again before the final draft went to the publisher.
(Barb edited the entire book for me). *And Jane read each of them at least twice. You know what? I'm getting tired of you guys!* (More laughter).

But I say all this just to let you know that if you do find a comma in the wrong place, or two periods at the end of a sentence, or no period at all . . . please be a "silent hero" and don't tell me about it. I really don't want to know.

I've been asked if I have another book in mind, and before I can answer, Jane will say, "NO!" (Still more laughter).

We sold just over 300 copies of *Silent Heroes* that day.

The day after launch I e-mailed each of our grandkids who helped, in one way or another, in the launch effort. Stacy, the only one who couldn't make it, was a freshman at Hope College on the west side of the state (Holland, MI) and had no transportation to get there.

Kevin, then a freshman at Lawrence Technological University, and who had his own transportation, and in his wonderful way with words, responded by saying,

Grandpa,

I wouldn't have missed yesterday's event for the world. I am so proud of you! I figured no matter how many times I said that in an email, it would be just a saying. But for me to be there I thought was a great way to show how proud I am! I can't wait to read the book!

Much love,
Kevin

Another note of note was from the daughter of one of the veterans of World War II. Her dad, Bob Graves, was a bomb diffuser who worked much of the time in the war zone defusing bombs that had not exploded. When his daughter, Sharon Troyer in Colorado wrote me, saying she now knew her father better and knew why he was always pretty much of a "loner." His "occupation" during the war could only be done by one person at a time, and he just always learned to do things by himself.

When I stated that during the introduction to my opening remarks at the launching, I mentioned it, without mentioning her name. Her note to me read,

Lowell—Thank you for making Veteran's Day so special for my dad. When I called him on that day to say I was thinking of him, he told me he had gone to your book-signing and he asked me if I was the one in Colorado who had said those things. He said he <u>knew</u> it was me and how proud it made him feel!

I think he is learning how valuable and unique his experience was and that others are benefiting from them—that they are a gift he can share with others.

Have a Merry Christmas and Happy New Year.

Sharon Graves Troyer

Another e-mail I received was from the "other" Lowell Thomas in Midland. I mentioned him in *So Far . . . So Good* and how we frequently got each other's mail when Jane and I lived in the city. In his pre-retirement years he was a chemist for The Dow Chemical Company. He and his wife, Jan, have become friends over the years.

Lowell wrote, in part, on March 13, 2005:

Just wanted to congratulate you on your book. I got a copy and have looked it over. There are several familiar faces. It is a good read and a very nice job of creating some history that otherwise would not have been noted. This is a great service to the characters and Midland history. We all thank you for doing that.

The only problem you have now is when you will write the next one. I'm sure there are many who will come forth with their story that wouldn't otherwise. I will have to get your autograph later as I was off hunting during the other times. Or maybe I could sign it with my left hand. Not!

Cheers,
Lowell & Jan Thomas

In response, I e-mailed back:

> *Thanks for your kind note and for purchasing the book. It has been a great experience with a few neat "twists." At one of the book signings, a lady in her mid-thirties said, "My grandmother has all your books and I want her to have this one too." Hey, if Granny wants to think I'm still writing at 112 (he was born in 1892), that's fine with me.*
>
> *My book is also listed on Amazon.com and under it says something like, "Those who have enjoyed this book will also enjoy . . ." and it lists books by authors of fifty years ago, including the late LT. Will it never end?*
>
> *Go ahead and autograph the book. Who will know? And say something like, 'To a great guy and a treat to know.' In my book presentations I've tried to make it clear that if anyone would want to call me, don't look in the Midland phone book. Only the name is the same.* (We had a Beaverton address and phone number at the time). I also suggested that he add), *and that 'he is a nice guy too, but not nearly as humble." I just hope we haven't created even more phone calls for you that should have been mine.*

That type of banter went on for years, and I have always had the highest respect for Lowell and Jan. I also find it ironic that Lowell's wife's name is Jan (undoubtedly Janice or Janet. We never knew), and the only thing that separates his wife's name and my wife's name is an "e."

Another interesting, but insignificant, occurrence happened from a doctor's office. Every time I would have a doctor's appointment, I would take one of my books along, pretending to read it, and carefully place it on the counter near the doctor as he/she entered and greeted me. (I sold five books in this manner, including those to nurses and office workers).

One was to a receptionist at a chiropractor's office in Gladwin. She purchased it for her father for Christmas. The first bill I received after Christmas, the receptionist enclosed a note which read, "Hi, Lowell! My dad loved the book and has read many of your books. He knows all about you and was very impressed with his gift! Thank you! Lisa." Thank you, Lisa, and all your dad knows about me is what is stated in the short bio on the back cover. But bless her heart. I knew her dad thought I was the "other" Lowell Thomas.

On another humorous note, after nearly all the books had been sold, I began going into Amazon.com on the computer, look up my book and purchase one or two used ones because they were less expensive than I could get them from the publisher. They always came to me brand new. Except one.

Early on, I had used my devious technique to sell one to my medical doctor. Later, he moved his practice to Holland, Michigan to be nearer to his aging parents. The "used" books seldom came from the same location. This one day I received one from Goodwill Industries of West Michigan. How did I know it was the one I had sold to my doctor? Because I had endorsed it, "To Doctor Steve . . . Lest we forget our silent heroes." And I had signed it. Jane said I should call him and say, "Hey Doc, I found your book." Someday I will cut that page out and give it to someone.

Of the 1,200 copies of *Silent Heroes* eventually printed, and was launched on November 11, 2004, by the time we entered the gates of Plantation Estates in mid-December, there were less than three dozen copies remaining.

It was decided not to have a re-printing. To do so meant a continual promotion program. Once was enough. I had been making public appearances in Midland and Gladwin Counties for over six months, pushing interest in the book. If they didn't sell after the first printing, a couple hundred books stacked in the spare bedroom, garage or pole barn, would not make for a gala decoration.

CHAPTER NINETEEN

Cherish your friends. You only have them for a lifetime.

Where there are ups, there also can be downs. 2004 was the year of Charley. Hurricane Charley, where dozens of homes in Plantation Estates were damaged or wiped out. We lost our carport, lanai (Florida's fancy name for a screened-in porch) roof and two beautiful palm trees next to the house. Actually, that's how we lost our carport and lanai. They blew over on them.

The roof was repaired almost right away, but the carport wasn't replaced until several months later. The palm trees were replaced with an orange and a grapefruit tree. They were producing when we arrived the following winter. Fortunately, the inside of the house was not damaged. In all, the damage amounted to about $16,000, $2,000 of which was our co-pay. Naturally, the insurance rates, if one could still get insurance, went through the roof (symbolically speaking). Many insurance companies left the state, taking with them the billions of dollars they had made prior to Charley.

Little wonder there was so much damage. In a news release in the Fort Myers *News-Press,* which I had read online on August 12, 2004, mentioned that the hurricane hit the Tampa Bay area with winds up to 120 mph, with heavy rain. Our Florida home is about 90 miles south of Tampa and it had devastating effects in our area as well.

CHAPTER TWENTY

When things look bad, look around the corner.
Things are about to look better.

"A year that was different, that's what it was. And it started off on a sad note." That's how the 2005 Christmas letter began. We were still suffering from the loss of Jane's oldest sister, Roberta. She died of a heart attack in Florida on December 9.

On a brighter note, I had entered an on-line writing contest. The first prize was $150, second prize, $50. Third prize was a book on how to promote one's book. That's what I won. But there were 174 entries so I felt I did rather well. I never read the entire book because I soon discovered I could have written it!

My entry was about how I became involved in writing, going back to my college days as a freshman at Western Michigan University in 1957. I called it:

A LITTLE ENCOURAGEMENT GOES A LONG WAY

As professor Woods handed back the essays, I couldn't help but notice the number of students around me who were receiving a "C-" "D" or "F." These were students who had been taking their fourth year of high school English just three months ago.

I hadn't taken an English class for over three years. Uncle Sam had seen to that. With dread, I sat waiting for the professor to drop my paper on my desk. Placing it face down, he smiled and turned away, delivering the bad news to the others. I shuddered.

Mustering up courage, I sat rubbing my fingers across the back of the paper, thinking perhaps the motion would somehow improve the grade,

*whatever it was. I had written about a trip I had taken from Camp Zama,
Japan, to Hiroshima four months earlier, where the first atom bomb to ever
drop in a war zone hastened the end of World War II. But this was peace
time, and over a decade had passed since that fateful day.*

*I wrote about a trip I had taken? I kept asking myself, "How could I do
that? Everybody takes trips and reading about them later is boring to say the
least. What have I done?"*

*Slowly, I turned over the corner of the paper where I thought the grade
would be. My eyes widened in disbelief as I saw the big red "B+."*

*Encouraged, my next paper for professor Woods was about various
customers I encountered on my part-time job at a local toy store. This time the
red lettering revealed an "A."*

*Showing the paper to my store manager, he encouraged me to send a copy to
the New York Toy Buyer's Guide. "Perhaps they will print it in their quarterly
Buyer's Guide," he said.*

*I forgot about having submitted it for nearly three months when I received
a letter, a copy of the publication and a check for $15. WOW! They even paid
me for it! I hadn't given that a thought. It doesn't sound like much now, but a
whole semester's college tuition was only $125 in 1957.*

*In the ensuing years I have written hundreds of articles for state and
national publications, for several newspapers and corporations in Michigan,
and have eight books to my credit.*

A little encouragement <u>really</u> goes a long way!

I entered a second online contest the following spring, entering a story
on how to promote one's book. This time I took first place with a check
for $25. (WOW!) I could never find out how many entries there were. I
would suspect about one. This aging memory doesn't recall the title, but
it must have been a whopper.

I also continued to write feature stories for the *Midland Daily News*. It
is something I truly enjoyed. I had been doing that since 1968.

And of course, there's the file full of short stories the world will
always suffer from because they were never given the pleasure of reading;
including the many stories submitted to magazines and have been rejected.
A real shame. I'm certain some of them were Pulitzer Prize winners. But
going back on my word again, as of this writing, I am in the process of
putting those short stories into book form and calling it, *Thomas Tidbits
for Today.*

Right after arriving at our Plantation Estates home in Ft. Myers in 2005, I heard about and readily joined the Gulf Coast Writer's Association. Meeting monthly, the Association boasted nearly 100 members. It was good belonging to a group of people with similar interests in writing. Soon I was installed as the assistant membership chairman, but gave it up the following year. It was a little awkward, being on the Board of Directors and being able to attend only four of the monthly meetings each year.

CHAPTER TWENTY ONE

Cry <u>with</u> someone. It's more healing than crying alone.

In the spring of 2005, we were thrilled by the visit of Nobu and Shimako Tomono, the Japanese friends we stayed with on the Chiba Peninsula, just south of Tokyo in 2001. They were such a delight. Again, we headed north with Japanese friends to the Mackinac Bridge, crossed the bridge and by boat to Mackinac Island. It was a wonderful day, but afraid we wore poor Nobu out. He was a little older than Jane and me and we were in out late 60s. Before we had completely crossed the bridge coming home, he was sound asleep in the back seat.

Nobu had been working on translating my book, *Silent Heroes,* into Japanese. He had even enlisted the aid of two of his friends. Ever so often he would e-mail me, announcing the progress, albeit slow.

I couldn't imagine why the Japanese would want to read it. It does not paint their World War II ancestors in a very pretty light. I was nine years old when the war ended, but I remember some of the atrocities performed upon American troops in the South Pacific and remember even more reading the history of the war in early textbooks. Plus, I had first-hand information from the subjects in my book. I had no idea what Nobu would do with such a document if he and his friends ever completed the project. And I don't think they did.

When I was writing the veteran's stories for the *Midland Daily News,* I would frequently e-mail a copy to our other Japanese friend, Michiko Takahashi, in Fukushima, 150 miles north of Tokyo. Michiko was about 40 at the time and it was evident that she had little or no information about World War II, nor was the topic studied in their textbooks in their schools.

But the pleasures of spring soon gave way to the pain of summer. It was August 25 and I had written on my laptop computer the following:

Here we go again (referring to my waiting room experience while Jane was undergoing her breast lumpectomy in 2002). *It began six weeks ago. We had old high school friends, Larry and Donna Swarthout, from Spring Lake (near Holland, MI) in for lunch. They also have a Florida home only two miles from Plantation Estates where we enjoyed the winters.*

As Jane slid up to the dining room table, she yelped and it was easy to tell she was in pain. She thought some cartilage had slipped in her knee. The bottom line was that x-rays would later reveal she had a cyst under her left knee cap.

Our friends, Donna and Larry Swarthout (Jane had dated him in high school), left right after lunch because they knew Jane's problem needed medical attention. They were right. Jane couldn't walk.

Fortunately, we were having the bathrooms in our home on the lake remodeled at the time, and together the carpenters and I got Jane into the office chair which had castors, and rolled her out the door, lifting her over the steps. I had driven the car up to the front door and together, we lifted her into the car.

The emergency room at the Midland hospital had been alerted and supposedly prepared for us. A wheel chair was wheeled to the front door of the ER, but nearly an hour passed before Jane got the attention she needed. He was a charming, good looking, personable doctor who seemed to have her best interests at heart. I am still not convinced of that.

He gave her prescriptions for pain and sent her home. This is where I made a mistake by not saying, "Hey, this lady can't walk. How will she get from the car into the house?" Looking back, it seems the doctor might have thought of that as well.

It was after six P. M. by the time we arrived home. Once again I drove up to the front door and helped Jane back onto the office chair on the sidewalk. The carpenters, of course, had left by that time. Knowing our neighbor from near Detroit was up for the weekend, I called upon him to help me lift Jane, chair and all, into the house. Living in the woods, without any other neighbor near us, I'm not certain what I would have done if our Detroit neighbors had not been there.

A few days later, Jane was in the same excruciating pain. Her pain prescription had lost its effectiveness. It happened on a day when the carpenters were not working. I called 911 for help getting Jane into the car. Eight people responded from the Billings Township Fire Department.

Fortunately, the docs in the ER became convinced this time that Jane should be hospitalized until she could walk out. Duh-uh! The next day, an orthopedic surgeon visited Jane in her hospital room and was dismayed that not even x-rays had been taken. Another unnecessary delay. But that was to reveal the cyst under her knee cap. A shot of cortisone was the temporary solution and a few days later Jane met the surgeon in his office and an appointment was made for arthroscopic surgery two weeks hence.

That brings us to this moment and to the waiting room at Midland hospital. Jane had had the same surgery on the knee several years ago and we know the healing process takes place rather rapidly. Our main anxiety is that she is completely healed prior to our European river trip which begins September 21, less than a month away.

But the anxiety of her last surgery was lacking. Fortunately! On July 7, 2002 I had been waiting in a different room while Jane had a lumpectomy for breast cancer. We thank God that nothing of that kind has since appeared on the horizon.

Jane recovered rapidly, and a month later we left, with our good friends, Dave and Jan Weissenborn, for Europe, and a riverboat cruise in that part of the world. After three fabulous days in Paris, we boarded a bus and headed for Luxembourg where we boarded the boat. When I say "we," it was just Jane and I. The day before we were to leave Paris, Jan suffered from food poisoning and had to stay under a doctor's care in the hotel room. They later caught up with us and the boat in Frankfort, Germany.

Traveling 738 miles down the Mainz, Seine, Rhine and Danube rivers, we passed through France, Germany, Austria and Slovakia and ended up in beautiful and enchanting Budapest, Hungary. It was a wonderful trip (Jan thought so as well once she left Paris).

While I intended to write up our experiences (As always, I took my laptop computer) and often went to the ship's library early in the morning to write. But the only thing I submitted to the *Midland Daily News* was one experience I alone had had in Paris. It went like this:

PARIS, THE CITY OF CULTURE, NINETY-EIGHT PERCENT AND THE EIFFEL TOWER

Paris, a city of ninety-eight percent. Ninety-eight percent smoke cigarettes. Ninety-eight percent use cell phones. And a massive number smoke cigarettes while using a cell phone. Another significant number drive motorcycles and motor scooters while smoking a cigarette, talking on a cell phone wedged between their cheek and their helmet-lining while darting like drunken mice through a maze, around those who are driving cars, trucks and busses. You know they are on their cell phones because their cigarettes are bobbing up and down like cold rain drops on a hot tin roof. The noise of the city drives out anything audible coming from the lips.

Before leaving for Paris, we had been warned about the French attitude toward Americans. "Don't wear a flashy sport shirt because they will know you are an American," some said. Others advised, "If the natives ask, tell them you are a Canadian." Since 9-11 I have proudly worn an American flag pin on the front of my Tilly hat, and I was warned to remove it before going in public in France.

I don't know what these advice-givers thought would happen, but I kept my flashy American shirt, adorned with colorful fish of all kinds and sizes, wore my Tilly hat with my American flag pin and even included my Michigan State University T-shirt on my trip to the Eiffel Tower.

I suspect nothing "happened" for a couple reasons; in the first place I was normally found in places where they were very receptive to taking my money, and secondly I was usually with a group of other people on our tour, and no one wanted to mess with a bunch of senior citizens from America. After all, those fighting Americans in our group, who once saved the French people from having to learn German sixty years ago, are all senior citizens. And we certainly weren't going to force them to learn English.

Paris is a city of two million people, with another eight million commuting from the suburbs to work . . . all at the same time. It was a wonder our tour bus, which seemed to have more square feet than a double-wide mobile home, could maneuver the narrow and sometimes tapered streets lined with small historical buildings which were built long before modern history said we needed wider streets to accommodate large vehicles.

And Paris wouldn't be Paris without the Eiffel Tower. Early on, during our three-day stay, I decided to make the journey to the top. My traveling companions decided not to. Little did I know how arduous that journey would be. It was our final full day in this city of ninety-eight percenters. Only a block from our hotel, the tower was an awesome sight, stretching vertically through the atmosphere the distance of more than three football fields. As I approached the ticket booth, I saw the sign that read in both English and French, "Approximately 30 minute wait." I could handle that.

Besides, that would give me an opportunity to observe people. But the sign wasn't even half right.

The "thirty-minute wait" meant to the ticket booth. Right on schedule, I bought my ticket thirty minutes later, and then waited in line another fifteen minutes for the elevator that would take me directly to the top. Well, not exactly directly as I found out. This elevator only went the first ninety-five feet. Way over two football fields to go to reach the top. At the ninety-five foot level one had to disembark, walk past the gift shop (those French entrepreneurs are no dummies), and wait in line another forty-five minutes.

The lines, both on the ground and at the ninety-five foot level wound around cattle-like stanchions much like those in a bank lobby. I thought, Why am I putting myself through this? I looked around for a way to return to the ground. I didn't see any signs in English or any arrows pointing downward. And I couldn't ask anyone about how to leave the stanchion and return to earth because no one around me was speaking English.

But if the U.S. Army taught me anything fifty years ago, it was to be patient. That was right after you hurried to get somewhere so they could test your patience. And it gave me plenty of time to observe people.

One of the first things I observed was that the French people have an affliction for affection. Everywhere one went people were hugging and kissing. I guess this is Paris. I don't mind this, but someone should remind them to get a room first. It was no different in line at the Eiffel Tower. At times it seemed like a contest to see which partner could extract the tongue from the other first. I guess this is French. Not that I noticed all that much. And the affliction wasn't relegated just to the young.

The couple in front of me had more grey in their hair than did I. But they had to have been half my age and acted like they were half theirs. They couldn't keep their hands, and mouths, off each other. In addition, they had with them four children, ranging from about four to twelve who loved to play in, around and over the metal bars separating the cattle-like lines of people. Perhaps that explained the premature grey hairs, and their immature, teenage-like actions in public might explain why they had four kids.

Finally, the cattle-like lines moved and we were herded into the waiting elevators for the ascent to the top.

The view was breathtaking, but I have been atop the Empire State Building in New York City, the Sears and Hancock buildings in Chicago and a 400 foot high structure in downtown Tokyo. Somehow the views are having their similarities. The "30-minute wait" from bottom to top to bottom, took just over two hours. Would I do it again? Sure, as long as I can soak up some French culture on the way to the top.

Oh, and I might have exaggerated about the ninety-eight percent of Parisians who smoke cigarettes. It is probably closer to ninety-six percent.

Eiffel Tower, Paris

CHAPTER TWENTY TWO

Life is good in a Joint Camp, and not even harsh on the lungs.

On November 14, 2005 I wrote on the same laptop, in the same hospital waiting room, the following:

Surgery waiting room, Midland Hospital Center. We knew it had to happen. Ever since that August day when her knee first went out, we knew we would someday end up here. We were just hoping and praying that it could wait until after our 19-day European river cruise (with three days in Paris), that had been in the works for nearly a year. We were so-blessed. It was a wonderful experience and making it even more-so was traveling with our good friends, Dave and Jan Weissenborn.

Dave, Jan, Jane and I had enjoyed many travels together, and it was because of that couple we settled in Ft. Myers during the winters. They already had a place there, and we had become acquainted when both Dave and I served on the Board of Directors of the former Teacher's Credit Union (now known at Member's First). Until their retirement, they were both teachers in the Bullock Creek Community Schools, located in Midland.

We had traveled to Europe together for the river cruise and to the Canadian Rockies on the domed train the following year.

But we did have our rules. For example, if either couple wanted to go off on their own to explore, or on a separate tour without the other, that was fine. This was agreed to from the beginning and was probably what kept us friends throughout the years on our travels.

Anyway, on our trip together through Europe, Jane would sometimes use a cane on the European city cobblestone streets during a walking tour. And sometimes she would just forfeit the tour because she knew she would end up in pain. The trip went well, however, partially because we were *able to change to a room on the river ship . . . . for a $50 fee . . . . that minimized walking up and down stairs.*

Her surgery date had been established nearly a month prior to the trip, and Dr. Bortel had injected cortisone in both knees a few days before we left.

After the trip, Jane began using pain killers more and more, which helped convince both of us that the surgery was necessary. However, a week before surgery, Jane convinced the surgeon that the knee he had designated for the replacement (the right) was less serious than the left. But we all knew the right knee would need the same total replacement as the one he is operating on as this is being written.

This was to be a long day. We arrived at the hospital at 5:30 a.m., at 6:00 the paper work and prepping began and at 6:45 Jane was wheeled into pre-op. Frankly, it is a pretty helpless feeling to watch a loved one being wheeled away on a hospital bed, knowing the next time you see them they will be groggy and shortly, perhaps, in a great deal of pain. One comforting thought was remembering that Dr. David Bortel had accomplished this feat over 2,000 times in the past.

As soon as Jane was taken away for surgery, I headed for the blood laboratory to give a small amount of blood in relation to the annual physical exam I had had two weeks ago. Since I had to fast for the blood work, I then rushed to the hospital cafeteria for a good breakfast.

Upon returning to the waiting room around 7:45 a.m., I found son Dave waiting. I knew he had been hunting with his pal, Jay O'Hara, near Chicago the previous week and I encouraged him to go to his office and return around 11:00 a.m. By then Jane would be out of surgery and perhaps even able to have a short conversation before her drugs took her off to la-la land again.

Two weeks prior to surgery we were invited to Joint Camp which is a large room just down the hall from Jane's room. I was suspicious at first, thinking it was a place where we would get something really good to smoke. Of course, they were talking about the joints in the body that were being replaced. About 25 people showed up and we learned what we had to do to help the patient after she/he returned home.

At 9:15 Dr. Bortel entered the waiting room to tell me that everything went to perfection. He had a very comforting manner about him and Jane and I liked him very much even at our first appointment with him.

Dave appeared right on schedule and while we were having lunch in the hospital cafeteria, a volunteer appeared to tell us Jane was now in her room and could have visitors . . . . whether she wanted them or not.

She was still groggy from the anesthesia, and as it wore off, the pain commenced. More pain killer was administered, both intravenously and by mouth. Sometimes it just wasn't enough. She said it wasn't a pain that came and went, it was a pain that came and stayed.

The second day was no better. It seemed that when pain medication was administered the nausea came back. When the nausea left, the pain came back. And so it went for most of the day.

Others in the same hospital wing who had had the same procedure the day before were being helped by a physical therapist and a walker, and were already walking, though slowly, out into the hall and back into their rooms. Whenever the therapist came into our room Jane was feeling nauseas. Finally, the pretty blond therapist came in knowing the situation, but Jane was the last one in the wing to take those first few steps and the therapist wanted to go home I'm sure.

With her hands on the walker, Jane forced herself up, the therapist holding onto a canvass belt she had fitted around Jane's middle. Still a bit dizzy and nauseas, Jane asked me to hold the pan in the event she was going to be sick.

As soon as she stood, hanging onto the walker I applauded, gave her an "Atta girl," and very nearly cried. She walked as far as the door of the room, turned around and headed back to the bed. At this point, the therapist placed her ailing leg into a form that mechanically moved it slowly up and down as she lay in her bed. It hurt her at first, but not as much as we both expected.

Each person who had had surgery the same day as Jane was all located in one area of E-Wing. There were about five or six, and each patient was asked to have a responsible person stay with them as much as possible. Despite my shortcomings, Jane selected me. I was also dubbed the "coach" for my patient by the nursing staff. The coach was the encourager and assisted with the physical therapy.

I kidded the nurses that I needed a T-shirt that said "Coach" on it. The next day they handed me a T-shirt with the name of the hospital on it and on a piece of tape had printed "Coach" and attached it to the sleeve. They have to have their lighter moments too.

We had prepared for Jane's return from the hospital by picking up all the throw rugs to make certain she wouldn't trip as she walked about the house using her walker. We also purchased a riser for the toilet seat and a sturdy plastic chair for the shower.

It was in the shower that I nearly met my demise the day after she arrived home. No, I wasn't in the shower with her. I was putting some laundry in the washer just through the door to the bathroom. She had said I might have to help her shave her legs, then after I began the laundry, and without telling me, she decided she could do it herself, sitting on the plastic chair.

Suddenly, I heard a "clunk." Fearing the worst, I went storming through the door to the bathroom, skidded across the floor, nearly slamming into the far wall, after sliding past the open shower door, while the hand-held shower did a dance around the shower stall. She had dropped it!

One of us got the shower turned off; I don't remember which of us. We stood there . . . OK, she sat there and we looked at each other. She, naked on the shower chair and me standing there soaking wet. Even the mirror across from the shower stall was dripping water. Then we both began to laugh and laugh and laugh. The incident, however, did relieve a great deal of the stress we had been under. I had to change my clothes and mop the floor before I could even assist her out of the shower.

Jane remarked later that she had no idea why she had not closed the shower door or why she didn't just reach up and turn off the water as soon as she had dropped the shower head. Drugs do funny things to the mind.

CHAPTER TWENTY THREE

In the rhythm of life we sometimes find ourselves out of tune.
But as long as there are friends to provide the melody,
the music plays on.

Onward and upward. 2005 witnessed us celebrating the retirement of Brother Bruce. He had been an educator in Montana for the past thirty years, most of it as an elementary principal in Clancy, a small community just outside Helena. We wanted so much to fly out from Michigan and surprise him on his big day. But it wasn't to be done.

In his earlier life, Bruce had had a tough time growing up. During his teen years, he had had a problem with Dad, who had come from the old school and whatever a parent wanted from a kid a parent got. Not Bruce, who had a mind of his own. Finally, between his junior and senior years of high school, he announced he was going to quit school and join the Army. All this is described in the first volume of *So Far . . . So Good*. And it was described so good that I won't go into details here.

Bruce and our parents finally agreed that he would come live with us and finish high school. It was my second year of teaching and my first year of teaching in Midland.

It worked out well and he graduated in 1963. Going through several phases after that; from "Jesus freak" on a motorcycle, to a college graduate with a M.S. degree plus dozens of graduate hours beyond his M.S., he ended up in the Montana Public Schools, married to Jeanette. Jeanette was his fourth wife, and the best thing that had happened to him in a long, long time.

In May, I sent him the following letter:

Yo Bro (and Broette),

HAPPY RETIREMENT!!! It's everything it's cracked up to be.

We would like to be with you on such an important occasion, but circumstances prohibit it. Frankly, we never imagined we would ever see 'baby brother' entering retirement.

You have come a long way since you lived with us and completed high school in 1963. We are extremely proud of those happenings in your life (okay, most of them). And had it not been for Jeanette entering your life, those happenings would have been much different, more difficult and perhaps not possible.

Enough said. There's already a lump in our throats. Last year we asked if you would visit us in Ft. Myers next winter if we could find some "cheap tickets." We found them! Nothing is "cheaper" than Frequent Flier Miles. We are willing to give you and Jeanette our Flier Miles account number so you can make the arrangements with a travel agent in your area. It is our gift to you both. Our extra bedroom in Ft. Myers is available for a week to ten days in February or early March, 2006.

Congrats to you both. Let us know if that will work for you.

Lowell and Jane

P.S. Of course, if you don't want to do this, all the blubbery above is null and void.

Fortunately, it did work out and is described in a following chapter.

CHAPTER TWENTY FOUR

Life is like a roll of toilet paper;
the closer you get to the end the faster it goes.

During the previous two years, our dear friend Nobu, still living on the Chiba Peninsula just south of Tokyo, had been working on translating my book, *Silent Heroes,* into Japanese. He had even enlisted the aid of two of his friends. Ever so often he would e-mail me, announcing the progress, albeit slow.

I can't imagine why the Japanese would want to read it. It does not paint their World War II ancestors in a very pretty light. I was nine years old when the war ended, but I remember some of the atrocities performed upon American troops in the South Pacific and remember even more reading the history of the war in early textbooks. Nobu is just a little older than I, so certainly he knew more about the war than did I.

When I was writing the veteran's stories for the *Midland Daily News,* I would frequently e-mail a copy to our other Japanese friend, Michiko Takahashi, in Fukushima, 150 miles north of Tokyo. Michiko was about 40 at the time and it was evident that she had little or no information about World War II, nor was the topic studied in their textbooks in their schools. I had no idea what Nobu would do with such a document if he and his friends ever completed the project.

2006 was a memorable year for a celebration . . . of sorts. I turned 70. Jane, who had never lied to me, to my knowledge, said she had tickets to see one of my favorite comedians at the Soaring Eagle Casino in Mt. Pleasant, forty miles distant. All my favorite comedians were dead; Bob Hope, Red Skeleton, George Burns, etc. I couldn't imagine who it might be. I didn't even like Jay Leno or David Letterman.

"But," she said, "on our way to the Casino we are going to stop at Buck's Run for a quiet dinner." Buck's Run, at a golf course, was one of our favorite restaurants on the way to Mt. Pleasant. OK, it wasn't quiet and we weren't going to the casino at all. She lied twice.

When we walked into the restaurant I was looking for a quiet table off in the corner somewhere. As I looked around the large dining room I saw only a few tables moved together, occupied by some group and a few single tables where couples were sitting. Attached to some of the chairs were helium balloons. In exasperation, Jane said, "See anyone you know?" I was still looking over the tables for someone I might recognize.

As we got nearer the line of tables with the balloons I was looking over, I heard, "Happy birthday, Dad/Grandpa." There was my whole family; two kids, their spouses and five grandchildren. I quickly forgave Jane for lying to me as she helped me pick my chin up off the floor. I was in shock! Never before had I been so surprised.

After we had a lovely dinner, Jane came out with a questionnaire titled *Gramp's Trivia, 70th Birthday Party*, for everyone to complete. It was over two pages long with questions asking for my mother's maiden name, the name of my aunt who gave me the family Edison record player, the name of the German band I played in through high school, the number of college degrees I had accumulated, the foreign countries I had visited over the years, number of books I had authored, shoe size, the name of our family dog forty years ago to what I was voted "best" in my senior high school yearbook, and on and on and on.

I don't remember if there was a prize for the most correct answers, but knowing Jane, there undoubtedly was. Whatever it might have been, I had the best prize of all; having a loving family around me on my 70th birthday.

But before the question and answer game began, Jane had everyone around the tables tell a story about their favorite memory of me. I was nearly in tears before it was over and was reminded of how much influence adults make on kids even without the adult knowing it.

They began telling me what I had meant to them over the years. It's nice to hear those things while we are alive because we surely won't hear them at our funeral.

We had five grandchildren, ages 13 to almost 21 (at that time), but the person who touched me the most was our 13-year-old granddaughter, Jennifer. Jennifer has always loved to write short stories and poems. I had often read her work and encouraged her to keep it up, even when I thought it was not very good. But she told me she had submitted a poem to a publisher and it was going to be in a book to be published that fall. Then she said, "Grandpa, it was your encouragement that made it possible." At that point my bucket was running over.

And it also told me something else. Little do we know what we say or do that will motivate or unmotivate someone.

CHAPTER TWENTY FIVE

Beginning of a Turkish Delight

2006 also held a wonderful experience in the form of another cruise. This time it was from Istanbul, Turkey through the Black Sea, with several stops on Greek Islands. Just as a matter of history, when I was writing the stories of veterans for my book, it was agreed that for each story with one picture of each veteran, I would receive the whopping sum of $75.

After all the stories had been published in the newspaper, the newspaper changed its system. It had been automatic that I would receive a check for the amount mentioned above. After that, I had to bill the paper for my services. I instantly gave myself a $50 raise, plus $10 for each photo after the first one. Several stories carried two or three photos. Anyway, I received nearly $1,000 for the six stories. Had I been able to find out what the going rate was, it might have been more. But I did it for more than the money; the satisfaction of being published.

As always, I took my laptop computer and wrote as we traveled. I then submitted the stories to the *Midland Daily* News following the trip. Following are the stories I submitted of our Mediterranean cruise:

EDUCATORS LEARN LESSONS OF LIFE

It was somewhat troublesome when, in the September 29, 2006 headline in the *Midland Daily News*, we read, "Explosion Shuts Down Natural Gas Pipeline From Iran to Turkey." And in the context of the story it read, "Officials . . . . said they believed the explosion was an act of sabotage . . . ." The dateline was Istanbul, Turkey.

Good grief! In three weeks, on October 23, we would *be* in Istanbul. It was also disturbing to refresh our global geography and to learn that only a few hundred miles south and east of Istanbul, was Lebanon, Syria, Iraq and Iran and the western mountains of Russia. Before, they had only been places on the map, to be read about frequently in the newspaper or to learn about from the television clips. Now, they had personal meaning.

It didn't help either, to learn that the same ship we would soon be boarding lost, mysteriously a few months ago, one of its passengers. It was assumed he fell overboard, but was never found.

But this once-in-a-lifetime trip had been in the planning stages for nearly a year and we decided neither saboteurs several thousand miles away nor a missing person was going to deter our trip. Besides, our government wouldn't allow a ship full of senior citizens to sail into harm's way . . . would it? Secretly, Jane and I both hoped we weren't making a mistake. But these former educators were about to learn some lessons.

Right on schedule, the sleek, blue and white KLM 737 from Amsterdam, with its 155 passengers, touched down gracefully on the concrete airstrip at Ataturk International in Istanbul.

Both of us being retired educators, we appreciated the lessons we were about to learn. Lesson number one: find out where your luggage will be discharged before an exasperating experience dims the day.

The "Baggage" signs led us to the luggage carousels. Only one out of three was operating, so we had to assume that we were in the right place. There was no sign to confirm it, however. At least none that we could interpret.

After forty-five minutes of watching everyone else's bags swirling around the carousel, ours not among them, the sickening thought that our bags didn't make it from MBS loomed largely on our minds. We finally asked an intelligent-looking gentleman if he spoke English. "Yes, I do," he smiled. (I think the American flag pin on the front of my Tilly hat told him he was about to assist a weary traveler from the States).

Asking if this was where the luggage from KLM Airlines was dispatched, our second lesson was that the KLM turnstile wasn't even in this part of the terminal. Duh-uh, the flight attendants on the plane might have announced that before landing. Either that, or they could update their public address system so the public on the plane could understand them. But it wasn't to be.

We finally found the right location, and by this time the carousel wasn't carouseling. Panic was looming. Thousands of miles from home and our luggage was somewhere between MBS and Istanbul. We were not alone in our plight. But there, off to the side, were our two suitcases, waiting for us . . . or for an airport attendant to take them to lost and found. I have never before felt such an urge to hug an inanimate object.

The Conrad Istanbul had no shuttle bus, and since we couldn't read the regular bus schedule in Turkish, and since so few people we tried to talk to could understand or speak English, our only other option was a Taxi. And there was another lesson to be learned. The Turks spell Taxi as "Taxsi." That seems right too.

Istanbul automobile drivers are the best in the world. They have to be. It's a matter of self-defense. We have ridden taxis (taxsis) in New York City, Chicago and downtown Tokyo, but the Istanbul drivers put them all to shame. And it appears that Istanbul has not yet heard of seat belts. At least there weren't any in our vehicle. If we had had a cell phone I would have called our kids to tell them to prepare to collect our life insurance.

To make matters worse, there were people running up and down the dotted lines that separated the lanes on the three-lane highway, selling everything from cut flowers to helium-filled balloons. The only sensible people seemed to be the police. They stayed off the highway.

But another lesson had to do with traffic lights in the city, and a lesson that American cities could learn as well. Attached to most of the traffic lights and about the same size was a lit, digital counter, counting down the seconds you had before you ran a red light. As the seconds got down to about five, cars behind you would begin honking to urge those in front of them to hurry up so they too could make the green light.

If we sometimes think security is tight in America, it is even more so in Turkey. And perhaps justifiably so, being so close to Iraq and Iran. As the taxi approached the drive to the Conrad Istanbul, we were stopped by security guards in front of a sliding iron gate. One officer questioned our driver while the other checked the trunk and walked around the car with a large mirror on a long rod, looking underneath. Satisfied we weren't terrorists (my beard might have profiled us) we were allowed to proceed to the front door.

We had deliberately arranged a night in Istanbul prior to boarding the *Brilliance of the Seas* so we could get some rest and to soak up some of the local culture. A part of the culture of which we were not aware might require some soaking up. Water. It is very poor coming from the faucets, and sometimes scarce. If you want water with your meal, it comes in bottles, just like you buy at the store. And it is not cheap. We were served, at a cost of eleven Turkish liras, a 1.5 liter bottle. We found out the next day that that is about $8. The Visa card was taking a bath.

Before heading for our ship the next day, we took a guided bus tour of Istanbul. More lessons for these former educators. One lesson we learned was that Turkey is a country of 14 million people, thirty percent of which live in Istanbul. And, according to our guide, is the youngest country in the world. *Whoa*, I thought, *this country dates back to before the time of Christ.* It was our guide's humorous way of saying that the average age of the people in Turkey is twenty-four. Somehow I find that hard to believe. But maybe that was before *we* arrived.

Our guide also noted that Turkey has only a 5% illiterate rate. I find that hard to believe also, but perhaps she knew that there were mostly Americans on the bus. And perhaps she knew that 14%, as of 2003, of American adults are illiterate. (Statistics from the Midland County Literacy Council).

One other little tidbit worth mentioning is the price of gas in Turkey, which borders on two of the richest oil producing countries in the world. Since I don't pretend to understand the metric system and even less, the Turkish lira system, I asked our guide. The answer was awe-striking . . . "Eight dollars a gallon in American dollars," she said with disgust. That prompted the next natural question. "Why so much when you are so close to the source?" I asked. "Taxes!" she answered. "Many people do not or cannot pay their taxes to the government, so we all pay to make it up." Gee, why didn't *our* government think of that?

Fortunately, the bus dropped us off right at the pier late in the afternoon. The *Brilliance of the Seas* was the largest cruise ship we had ever been on . . . or even close to. Even larger than the troop ship I had sailed on across the Pacific fifty years ago. And certainly much prettier. We later learned that it held 2,100 passengers and 900 crew members. It held more people than there were in our home town where we grew up in southern Ionia County. More about the ship later.

At 8:00 p.m. on October 24, the *Brilliance of the Seas* slipped out of its moorings and headed on a southwest course through a small strait between the Black Sea and the Aegean Sea, heading for the island of Mykonos, Greece; a couple hundred miles south of Athens and the Greece mainland.

The Port of Mykonos is a beautiful city on the seashore and epitomizes the post card image of the Greek islands, with their dazzling white buildings offset by bright blue church domes, while golden beaches meet an aquamarine sea. Until one gets closer to the island, the buildings on top of the mountains look as though they were snow covered. Logic told us it wasn't snow. The mountains weren't very high, and the temperature on this late October day was in the 70s.

Our first land excursion, however, wasn't on Mykonos at all. About 300 of us were herded to a smaller ship at an adjacent pier and transported thirty minutes southwest, to the tiny island of Delos. This was to be a lesson in irony.

The reason for the visit to Delos was to observe the ancient ruins of a civilization demised 2,000 years ago. The homes were constructed of stone and marble and one could see the rooms of the buildings as they stood so many years ago. It seems that the Romans from another island came and obliterated all the people; men, women and children, then didn't even want the island for their own. And there stands the ruins over the centuries.

The irony lesson came when the crew of this small ship warned its passengers that there were no rest rooms on the island and that one should best use those on the ship before we docked. They announced this message a couple times in the half-hour it took to reach the island. Then, as we disembarked, they handed us a bottle of water. Am I missing something here?

BIBLICAL TIMES AND STUNNING SEASCAPES

Leaving Mykonos, we headed northeast, back to Turkey and to the tiny seaport city of Kusadasi. It is amazing how easily the captain of the ship maneuvers this 90,000 ton ship into such small spaces.

Kusadasi is nestled on the western coast of Turkey and contains history dating before the time of Christ.

We couldn't help but notice that uniformed armed military men were at various intervals along the streets. They carried both rifles and side arms. Asking the right question, we learned that the general population has more confidence in the military than the police; therefore, the presence of the military.

After a lengthy climb up a flat stone walkway we came to the house where it is said that the Virgin Mary lived out her later years. The building was made of brick and stone with a dirt floor and was actually in great shape for its supposed age. Inside were candles burning and two nuns who kept the foot traffic flowing smoothly through the house.

Hundreds of Christians visit the House of Mary daily, we were told. It's not only a place of pilgrimage for Christians, according to the literature, but also for Muslims who honor the Virgin Mary as the mother of "Jesus, the prophet."

On the way back to the bus there were shops lining the walkway where local merchants were hawking their products. Two young men approached and wanted to sell me a book about Ephesus. Since we were heading there next I wanted one . . . . but not at the price they were hawking for a fifty-five page book with pictures. Somehow $50 seemed a bit much. After several minutes of haggling, I purchased the book for $6. Then the guy asks for a one dollar tip. I informed him I didn't tip for buying a book, and got away with it. I probably could have gotten it for three dollars, but haggling over price isn't one of my strong suits.

Our next stop would be Ephesus, from which came the book of the Bible, Ephesians. It was a veritable haven for archaeologists. Over a distance of several hundred yards, the city is being reconstructed. Many of the walls and columns remain as they were in biblical times. And it is expected that the digs will continue for another hundred years before the total city will be uncovered.

The first people began settling in Ephesus around 3000 BC and is thought to be the most ancient city in the world. It was once the second largest city of the Roman Empire.

The most memorable structure was the open-air theatre with a seating capacity of 24,000. The theater looks much like the end section of a huge football stadium, except the seats are made of flat stones and marble. And the theater is carved out of a hillside, making it easer for the seats to stay in place. This is also where, according to the literature, the Apostle

Paul preached to the multitudes. It is also said that it was constructed for maximum acoustics. After all, the only sound system in Paul's day was the natural voice.

Just being there, where so much history once took place, left us awestruck.

Our ship, the *Brilliance of the Seas* once again headed south, passed Mykonos and docked at the beautiful Greek Isle of Santorini. A tour bus showed us part of the island, and then dropped up off in the town square. From there we were guided on a walking tour to other scenic parts of the city.

Jane and I had signed up for this walking tour because the travel brochure stated it was a "moderate walk" with only about forty stone steps to climb. This was important to us because Jane had had a complete knee replacement less than a year ago and we know the other knee was due for a replacement within the next few months.

Either the brochure had a typographical error or the responsibility of the person who counted the steps should have been transferred to someone else. The "forty stone steps" turned out to be closer to "140 stone steps." About thirty steps into the climb, Jane's knees told her she had reached the summit.

We returned to the square where we did a rather quick shopping tour, a cup of Greek coffee, then off to the cable cars that would return us to the bottom of the mountain where our bus waited to transport us to the ship.

One thing the travel brochure failed to mention was the numerous steps, uphill, to the cable car. And there was no other way to get there except to walk.

Rounding the southern end of the Greek Islands, the *Brilliance of the Seas* steamed northeastward to the seaport of Dubrovnik in Croatia. In our youth, Croatia was known as Yugoslavia.

Croatia's coast is a stunning seascape of rare beauty where pristine beaches and deep blue waters merge into the Mediterranean Sea. As in most of the Mediterranean, little limestone villages cling to the hillsides, allowing merchants the use of the coastline for business purposes, mostly tourism.

According to the brochures, Dubrovnik is a " . . . perfectly preserved old town, is unique for its marbled-paved squares, cobbled streets, tall houses, churches, palaces, fountains and museums, all cut from the same light colored stone." This time the brochure was correct. It was truly a delightful town. Its streets and lanes were blessedly free of vehicular traffic.

Once being there, it is easy to understand why people's homes and many shops are built into the hills and mountainsides. That's about all there is . . . hills and mountains. Very little flat land, except along the coast.

VENICE, THE CITY OF ROMANCE?

Venice . . . the home of the romantic. Or so it's said. Entering the large canal leading to the city, it was obvious the city is built on islands created by small canals. Neighborhoods are connected by walk bridges . . . 400 altogether we learned.

Boats on the main canal in Venice are akin to cars and trucks on Eastman Avenue in Midland. There is every kind, size, color and description of boat imaginable. Some go fast, some go slow, and some are just plain in the way. Where we go anywhere in Midland we wish to go, we go by car. In Venice, they go by boat.

Via the internet prior to the trip, we had purchased tickets for the first afternoon for a tour of a glass blowing factory and a hand-made lace demonstration. Jane did fall for a small hand-blown vase, but nothing caught her eye in the lace place. She did mention, however, that if my mother were still living, one of the beautiful lace-edged handkerchiefs would be appreciated by her in her old age. I didn't have the heart to mention to Jane that I spotted one I thought she (Jane) would appreciate. But then, I didn't want to say anything where she thought I was comparing her age to my mother's.

From the glass blowing and lace places, the small boat brought us back to our ship. We were late getting back because we were late in leaving. It seems that as we were about to dock in Venice, a group of protesters formed on the pier and were finally escorted away by the local gendarmes.

We learned they periodically do a protest demonstration against large ships because they churn up the relatively shallow canal, disrupting the watery environment at the bottom.

We were so late in getting back to the ship we didn't have time to eat in the main dining room so we grabbed a quick bite in the cafeteria and hurried to our evening tour on the waters.

The gondolas went out in groups of six. Sometimes side-by-side but often in single file through the narrow canals. Each gondola also carried a bottle of cheap champagne and paper cups for its occupants to enjoy during the forty-five minute voyage.

Each gondola seated six people and every sixth gondola also carried a singer and an accordionist. There were four of us in our gondola plus the two musicians. They were great! It was just like in the movies. The handsome, suave, male tenor, to our untrained ears, could have just come from Broadway.

It got awkward, however. It is difficult to applaud with a camera in one hand and a paper cup of champagne in the other. We soon learned to express our appreciation with, "Bravo, Bravo," and raising our cups.

Again, we were impressed by how people got around (by boat), even by water taxi, to do their shopping, eating out, etc. As the gondolas glided noiselessly around the watery streets, we passed shopping centers, restaurants and hotels. The residents had to get to them either by boat or by one of the hundreds of walk bridges.

We had opted for the evening gondola trip rather than the daytime trip the next day. Why? I haven't a clue, unless Jane hoped to spark something in me she might not have observed for awhile. It *was* rather romantic. However, because it was dark and in some places darker than others, even the flash on the camera couldn't bring the scene to life.

So by taking the evening gondola ride, we not only didn't have a good snapshot to show for it, but we later learned we also missed a lobster dinner in the main dining room aboard ship. How's that for romantic!

The second day in Venice we opted, along with many others, to leave the ship and fend for ourselves. The usual street vendors lined the sidewalks with their inexpensive souvenirs.

Then we discovered something quite by accident. We found a narrow side street that went to who knew where? Being in an exploration mood, we were to soon find out. That street lead to another, then another, and soon we were in the middle of a small metropolitan area with its flat stone sidewalks and shops that sold quality merchandise. There were neither cars nor boats. It was strictly a pedestrian traffic.

We wandered the streets and through the shops for over an hour and ended up in St. Mark's Square. The name meant nothing to me until we saw hordes of people and thousands of pigeons. Then I remembered seeing this feathery scene in many pictures and movies.

Jane and I sat at a small table in front of one of the many open-air restaurants and enjoyed a glass of wine while watching the people . . . and the birds. It was obvious the pigeons went there to eat and the people went there to feed them. The birds were so tame they would sit on one's hand, arm and head if one let them. And many children did, while their parents watched in awe.

One thing to be said for the pigeons . . . they were certainly well trained. The open-air restaurant area in which we sat also sat at least two hundred small tables where people could sit, as we were, enjoying the environment and the ambiance. Not one of those tables or the two small chairs with each, contained a drop of bird droppings. And many of the lovable birds were perched on light poles overlooking the tables.

At one point a pigeon's feather floated to the ground near me. I picked it up and stuck it in my Tilly hat. Doing that, I remembered telling my grandchildren when they were small, "Everyone needs a feather in their cap once in awhile." Then I would explain the meaning of that clever bit of pseudo-philosophy.

It was good that our ship was so tall . . . twelve decks (stories) altogether. The tall ship, sticking up higher than most of the buildings, was our guiding beacon back to a welcome rest in our room on the ninth deck.

I also received some welcome news from the captain of the ship. A few days earlier, I had gone through the channels to ask him for an interview. His aide called, saying the captain wanted to meet with me the next day. I would speak with him on our way to Naples.

The interview is written up in a later story.

NEARING NAPLES AND ROAMING IN ROME

Bidding Venice a fond farewell, the *Brilliance of the Seas* slid from its berth at 3:00 p.m., headed south along the eastern shores of Italy, beginning its 840 mile journey around the southern boot of the peninsula, then north to Naples.

It has been warm up until now, with the temperatures in the high 60's to low 70's. Checking the internet frequently at home, it told us the weather was going to be thunderstorms most of the trip. To this point, we have had sprinkles parts of two days. The rest of the time it has been beautiful. Meteorologists have the same problem in this part of the world too.

As we headed north along Italy's western coast, the temperature dropped into the high 50's. Still, for the first week of November, we new it must be warmer than at home.

The *Brilliance of the Seas* bellied up to the pier at Naples at 8:00 a.m., two days later. But we didn't stay in Naples for long. We had opted for a nine-hour bus trip along the Amalfi Coastline, skirting the southern flank of the Sorrento Peninsula.

On the way, we drove along in the shadows of the mysterious volcanic, 4,000 feet of Mt. Vesuvius. According to our guide (and the scientists he quoted), Mt. Vesuvius erupts every forty years. The last major eruption was in the 1940s. Mr. Guide Man assured us that, even though it was long overdue, the mountain would not erupt while we were there. He knew that because he hated scientists because they were wrong too often.

The scenery along Almalfi Drive is the most spectacular of anyplace we have ever been. The towering cliffs come straight up out of the sea. On top of cliffs people have built homes, restaurants, hotels and other businesses. The same goes for the valleys in between the cliffs. Villages have sprung up from these businesses spawning the tourist trade.

One of those villages is the fabled town of Sorrento. This delightful little town has a marvelous view of Naples Bay.

Positano, a pretty fishing village, has become a colony of artists and writers and their wares are in abundance in the shops. The picturesque seaside resort of Amalfi lies at the mouth of a deep gorge where we stopped for lunch at a local restaurant on the Amalfi Coast. Of course, the menu was all Italian and written in same, so we had no choice but to eat what was put before us. I still don't know what it was, but it was delicious.

During the nine hours there was ample time to shop the shops. We will undoubtedly receive a "thank-you" note from our Visa card company.

One of the miracles of the journey was our bus driver, Luigi. How he ever manipulated the twists and turns along this coastal highway was a marvel. It seemed to me that some of the sharp curves would not accommodate such a large vehicle. Luigi did it even while meeting a car on the turn. Often we were either going up hill or down. But Luigi did it.

Our next stop was Rome. However, Rome is not on the coast and we had to make port at Civitavecchia. (Anyone who can pronounce that on the first try should e-mail me and I'll fire back a note of congratulations).

But Civitavecchia was the way to Rome, an hour-and-a-half distant by bus.

Driving along the super highway toward Rome was not at all unlike driving I-75 to Flint; with its two lanes going in each direction, rolling farm land, rows and rows of grape vines, pine trees that shoot straight up with branches that sprout out only at the top (the natives call them "umbrella trees), and the ever-visible olive trees. Along the way were, to our surprise, palm trees (as there were in most of the Mediterranean countries).

OK, only like driving along I-75 was it the same . . . except I-75 isn't nearly as smooth a highway.

Of the many bus tours available, we had opted for the tour of Rome called "Panoramic View of Rome." It was somewhat of a mistake and gave true meaning to the word "panoramic." We saw a little of everything but not a whole lot of anything. It would have been nice to have gotten out and toured the inside of the Coliseum, but all we could do was snap a picture from the bus window as we zipped passed.

The highlight, however, was when we had forty-five minutes to visit the Vatican. Unfortunately, we did not have time to go inside. There were blocks and blocks of lines of people waiting to do so, and we had to get back to our "panoramic view."

But just being in the same courtyard which, on special occasions, holds hundreds of thousands of people waiting to get a glimpse of the Pope, was a special occasion for us as well. The Pope didn't make an appearance while we were there. He probably knew we were Protestants.

The most amusing thing we saw in all of Rome was the teenie-tiny cars. Because of the traffic, it was good they were so small. And they undoubtedly got sixty miles to the gallon with a good tail wind. In an accident, however, it would be like riding in a cardboard box.

Jane and I decided they would be a good thing for our country too, except it would take two trips to the supermarket just to haul home the groceries . . . providing one of us stayed home to begin with.

THE CAPTAIN AND HIS SHIP

At 46, Captain Petter (Peter) Sundet is single and looks very much like the kind of person you would want as the commander of a ship on the high seas; calm, assuring and very much in control of his surroundings. His office on board looks very much like an office anywhere; shelves lined with books (relating mostly to the sea and its navigation thereof), a kidney-shaped mahogany desk, a telephone and two computers.

Sundet is Norwegian. He served his mandatory term in the Norwegian Navy in the mid-70s and has since earned his Navigation Officer's and Master Mariner's license. In 1987 he began his career with Royal Caribbean. He has commanded six cruise ships for Royal Caribbean International, and has been at the helm of the *Brilliance of the Seas* since it was first launched four years ago.

The best part of his job, he says, "Takes place on the bridge to maneuver the ship into the canals where it is finally docked along side the pier." One has to marvel as to how a person, such as Captain Sundet, can slip the 90,000 ton craft up next to the pier as quietly and gently as though he was parallel parking his car on Main Street. "They don't like it if you bang into their docks," he chuckles.

Another thing he likes about his job is the interaction with the passengers. This he also does with skill, making everyone feel at home even though they may be thousands of miles from it. Speaking with several crew members during the cruise, it was obvious they viewed him as just that; the captain of the ship, and they spoke with reverence.

A true challenge for the Captain is dealing with so many authorities in so many different countries. These often consist of things such as public health, security, etc. "Every country has different rules," he claims. Captain Sundet has to know them all.

When time permits, he likes to go ashore at the different ports. Mostly, he likes to jog a couple miles to temporarily take his mind off the job. "It also keeps me healthy," he admits.

Captain Sundet does have his favorite ports: Venice, Stockholm, Barcelona, Vancouver, Singapore, Hong Kong and New Orleans (although he hasn't been there since Katrina). The captain does get around a bit.

The best times aboard ship, according to Sundet, are the nights in the Caribbean. "Not all nights," he says, "but sometimes when you are under the stars and moon, alone and far from home, you can feel a closeness about yourself. It's just a feeling I like. It makes you feel how very insignificant you are in such a vast universe."

The worst times are the storms at sea. "I have never felt in danger, but have felt that I was in constant control because I have so many human and technical resources from which to draw." He would still like to be able to eliminate them.

The *Brilliance of the Seas* is the length of three football fields, takes on 3,530 metric tons of diesel fuel to move the mammoth through the waters of the world. In fact, it takes nearly a gallon of fuel to move the craft only 45 feet.

To move the ship at a top speed of 24 knots (27.6 miles per hour), it burns 215 tons of fuel per day.

In addition, the ship uses, in a typical week, 18,450 fresh eggs, 12,500 pounds of fresh vegetables, nearly 12,000 pounds of fresh fruit, 785 gallons of ice cream, 550 pounds of lobster, 31,345 pounds of chicken and the list goes on and on.

Probably one of the best innovations on the *Brilliance of the Seas* was the hand sanitizing dispensers at the entrance to each dining area and at other locations around the ship. They were motion-sensitive and by placing one's hand under the nozzle, a few drops would be dispensed onto the hand. It gave everyone a peace of mind that they weren't spreading dreaded germs around the ship.

The captain has 900 people working for him and on any given cruise must accommodate 2500 guests.

Smiling, Captain Sundet says, "The best people in the world work for me."

THE FRENCH RIVIERA AND PISA

When we awoke on our 12th day aboard the *Brilliance of the Seas,* we were greeted with the brilliance of sunlight creating shimmering ripples on the northern Mediterranean. We also realized the ship was not moving. Walking out onto our balcony on the ninth deck, we saw a wonderful little village nestled in a shallow valley between the ridges of a sloping mountain range. It was Villefranche in southern France, better known as the French Riviera.

Villefranche is a busy little town with its yellow, red and pink pastel stucco houses that crawl up and down the hillside. Waterfront cafes line the main street where luxury yachts tie up, waiting for their occupants to command their bows.

Villefranche is also close to Nice (pronounced Niece), Monte Carlo, and Cannes. We had originally signed up for a ground trip to Monte Carlo because the travel brochure rated it as "moderate" in the walking department. But after our experience on Santorini, which also had "moderate" walking listed (and was far from it), we cancelled Monte Carlo.

There were other tours mentioned in the brochure, but we decided to go it on our own. Because of the size and/or depth of the harbor, the ship anchored about a mile off shore and took passengers to the pier via tender, a small, covered craft holding only 120 passengers at a time.

Arriving on land, we walked a short distance to a shuttle trolley and rode to the bus depot. We decided to be adventurous and take a bus to Nice, only 20 minutes away. Besides, we didn't have to be back on the ship until 7:30 in the evening. That would give us plenty of time to get lost and still return on time.

Nice might be nice, but we were not much impressed. From the bus depot, we walked several blocks in every direction, only to find Nice just another busy metropolitan city. We thought it's not necessary to travel thousands of miles from home to see this, so we returned to the bus depot once again for the ride back to Villefranche.

This return visit made our day. We shopped the open-air shops where Jane purchased a hand-woven basket; just the right size for a plane carry-on. It seems the little souvenirs were piling up.

Returning to the main street, we stopped at an open-air restaurant for lunch where we could watch the shimmering sun make sparkles on the harbor. The menu was printed in French, but with English descriptions of each dish underneath. Jane ordered some sort of spaghetti dish and I decided to have only an appetizer (knowing her spaghetti would be more than one person could eat).

On the menu I spotted my very favorite . . . escargot . . . a dozen of them. I know that escargot is snails and I've eaten them whenever I can, but I've never had them served still in the shell. Now that was a new adventure! With a tweezer-like tool for holding them, I coaxed the morsel out of its shell with a small fork. The snails were some of the best I've ever eaten. Of course, Jane's spaghetti was good too. Only to be expected so close to Italy.

That evening the *Brilliance of the Seas* steamed out of the harbor at Villefranche and backtracked across the northern tip of the Mediterranean Sea to Italy. This would be our last stop before sailing for Barcelona to catch the first of our three flights home; Amsterdam to Detroit to MBS.

While we ate dinner in a little café on the ship, we watched the glimmering lights of Monaco fading in the distance, knowing we would probably never again reach these shores.

The "umbrella trees" formed a canopy over the highway as the bus sped through the beautiful countryside of Tuscan and into the town of Pisa. Because of the logistics, the bus had to use a parking lot about a half-mile from our destination; the Leaning Tower of Pisa.

It was a pleasant walk through a charming neighborhood, however, and ever so often we would catch a glimpse of the tower over the trees.

A high wall goes around the grounds where the Tower sets near a huge, beautiful Catholic church that was built in the early 9th century. Along the wall were the street vendors hawking their wares of watches, purses, cheap plastic tower statues, etc. At least, once you said no to them, they left you alone. But somehow it stole some of the dignity of such a wonderfully historic place.

Once inside the walls it was easy to see the sixteen degree tilt of the Tower. Taking the usual pictures with our digital camera, I could view the shots immediately. I found that the Tower was perfectly straight in my first couple pictures. My brain apparently didn't like seeing leaning buildings and I subconsciously tilted the camera to straighten the Tower.

Fortunately, we did not have time to climb the 194 steps to the top so that took care of the decision, *Should we or shouldn't we?*

As the bus made the return trip to the ship in Livorno, we experienced a beautiful Italian sunset, realizing the sun was also setting on a wonderful two weeks aboard Royal Caribbean's *Brilliance of the Seas.*

Among other things, we had roamed Rome, had eaten Pizza in Pisa, and it was nice to have been in Nice, but we were ready to head toward that sunset.

All that night, all the next day, and the next night we steamed westward toward Barcelona where our 3800 mile cruise would end and where we would catch our first flight toward home.

There's still no place like it.

Having crossed the Atlantic and landing safely once again on American soil in Detroit, we felt we were home. Not quite. The last 45 minutes of our journey would take longer than the flight from Barcelona to Amsterdam to Detroit.

In a slight fog, the DC-9 lifted off the runway in Detroit heading for MBS. Just ten minutes away, the pilot made a brave, though disappointing decision. With an apology he told us over the intercom, "Ladies and gentlemen, safety is always our main concern and MBS is socked in with a very heavy fog. We are returning to Detroit."

We had been away from home for two weeks and had been up (counting from the time we had arisen in Europe six hours earlier than Michigan time) for twenty-four hours with only short cat-naps on the flights. We had counted off each of those eight hours across the Atlantic, now we were so close . . . but it wasn't to be.

Northwest Airlines put us up in a comfortable Comfort Inn near the airport with vouchers for two meals, and the following day we finally landed safely at MBS. It was truly good to be home.

Leaning Tower of Pisa

CHAPTER TWENTY SIX

Honest criticism is hard to take . . . especially from a relative,
a friend, an acquaintance, or a stranger.

Having written feature stories for the *Midland Daily News* for the past forty years, and had sold a story to *The Grand Rapids Press* and having sold a story to the Dow Corning Corporation about one of their former employees, I tried to venture out to the Ft. Myers *News-Press*. The *News-Press* "slightly" outnumbers the *Midland Daily News* in circulation about 17,000 to 93,000, so I thought it would be another feather in my cap to be published in the *News-Press*.

Working under a world of logic, I began by contacting the "Veteran's Editor" and told her briefly about my book and that I had written fifteen interviews with combat veterans in our Florida mobile home park, including three people who had grown up in Hitler's Germany and one person who had actually been placed before a Russian firing squad at ten years of age following the war. And that many of the veterans were permanent residents of Ft. Myers. "World of Logic" lost.

As is normal in large communication organizations, I was referred to another editor, then another (who makes decisions in such organizations? I wasn't asking to change the Constitution of the newspaper!). After at least a dozen E-mails and another dozen phone calls back and forth over a period of over two years, they (whomever "they" are) decided not to use my stories.

I e-mailed back, stating how disappointed I was that a local newspaper was not interested in local people who had helped make it possible for them to print their newspaper in English (instead of German or Japanese). I didn't make any friends at the *News-Press* that day. But I didn't cancel our subscription.

On the brighter side of writing, which was consuming much of my time by now, and enjoying it thoroughly, e-mails kept coming in response to my feature stories in the *Midland Daily News*. This time it was our cruise through the Panama Canal. Marion Newman, a prominent resident of Midland and a person who had crossed my path so many years ago I couldn't remember which path it was, and who had sent her message to one of the editors of the MDN, asking them to forward it to me. (Whew! How's that for a sentence from a writer?).

In part, Marion stated, *"I am really enjoying the Lowell Thomas account of their travels. Many Midland area residents are world travelers, as I am, and like to read about others' experiences. Thanks for the good reading."*

I was flattered, partly because many Midland area residents <u>are</u> world travelers, thanks to The Dow Chemical Company and to Dow Corning, both of whom have their world headquarters in Midland. I was also flattered because the Newman's are such respected people in the community even though I couldn't remember why.

But along with the good can also be some not-so-good. By this time I was a member of the Gulf Coast Writers Association (GCWA) and through a tip from another writer, learned that the Banyan Tree Books & Café in Ft. Myers welcomed authors to be available to sell their books during the lunch period.

WOW! What a break, I thought. The Banyan Tree Books & Café was a small restaurant and used book store located under a humongous banyan tree (where else?) in Ft. Myers. Thus it was, after making the arrangements by phone and meeting the owners the day before my sale of *Silent Heroes,* which would surely be a hit, I learned that the owners kept 40% of the sales, the author 60%.

It was fortunate I sold only two books, losing only $15.

CHAPTER TWENTY SEVEN

If you can smile when things go wrong,
you have someone in mind to blame.

The following informative letter was sent to Bruce and Jeanette in two separate e-mails on March 27 and March 31, 2007 from our winter home in Ft. Myers. Why I kept it in my files I have no idea. Perhaps just to lengthen this chapter. I called it *The Saga of the Rat Patrol.*

We are having a personal battle with a varmint! One morning we got up and found that something had chewed around the door to the lanai and along the weather-stripping of the door.

Well sir (mam), we began our fight to the finish. I got some D-con and placed it in conspicuous places. Next day the poison had been visited, but no signs of fresh meat. So I went to the local ACE Hardware and got some "Stick-em," a heavy glue laced with a peanut butter odor in a little plastic tray. NOW we got'em. Wrong! We looked all over for it and good friend and neighbor, Dave Weissenborn, found it wedged between the dish washer and the wall. He pulled it out and it was covered with grey hair . . . ouch! But no varmint.

Then I re-read the package of D-con and it mentioned "for mice." Nothing said about rats. Being the ever-clever person I am, I nailed two "Stick-em" trays to a board three feet long and placed it in front of the door. And being the ever-clever varmint, we have seen only his droppings since.

Yesterday I bought a rat trap, baited it with peanut butter, but last night proved no better than anything else we've tried. NOW IT'S WAR! Wish I was ever-clever enough to know what to do now. But one of these days . . . he is going to make a mistake. And that's why I have a shovel!

The nailed-down sticky traps didn't work. He/she (not sure) never went back to them. The rat trap with peanut butter didn't work. I knew the little sucker liked the D-con because it kept disappearing from the little tray thingy.

So I used fresh peanut butter laced with mouse D-con. Didn't work either. Someone said it was probably a fruit rat. Ever-clever me thought a piece of fruit might be the key. WRONG AGAIN!

Then out of the blue he appeared. As we were watching TV two nights ago, I got up from my easy chair, glanced down, and there he was, with his butt and tail showing from under my chair. Good grief, this could be easy, I thought. I went to the shed, got my leather work gloves (if he was going to bite me he was going to have to go through leather). Then Jane brought me the needle-nose pliers.

Would you believe he/she was still there . . . under the chair? Hadn't moved and I didn't know if he/she was dead or alive. I took the pliers and quickly grabbed him/her by the tail, just behind the butt. He/she squealed (guess I pinched a tad hard), and with all my might I slammed him to the floor. TAKE THAT YOU RAT! Then I picked him up with the pliers once again, rushed him/her outside and slammed him/her two more times on the concrete carport floor.

He/she (not sure) was smaller than a normal rat, but several times larger than a mouse. My theory is that he/she (not sure) didn't eat enough mice D-con to kill it, but just enough to partially knock him out.

End of the continuing saga of Rat Patrol. Tarzan wins again!

CHAPTER TWENTY EIGHT

Sometimes the old fashion way is the best way.

It is strange how some things can spark a thought, even when it's least expected. Around the 4ᵗʰ of July in 2007, I was reading something about patriotism in our country, or lack thereof, and I was prompted to write the following. I sent a copy of it to Brother Doug because he was a part of the thought, and sent a copy to a couple close friends. It wasn't until two years later that I sent it to the Midland Daily News, along with an interview I had done on a World War II veteran. Both items were published on the same page. For what it's worth, it went like this:

TAPS . . . THE OLD-FASHIONED WAY

It was the same old-fashioned Memorial Day Parade, starting at the high school, going down Main Street, and then school-bussed to the edge of town to the cemetery. The whole affair didn't take long, perhaps an hour including the bus ride. At its peak, the population of this tiny town was less than 3,000,

I was a senior in high school in 1954, had been playing the cornet since fifth grade and had been doing this annual parade thing with the high school band for the past four years. I had also played Taps each year at the cemetery, ending the ceremony.

It had always been an honor because only the best cornet/trumpet players in the fifty-piece band were given this prestige.

But this year was different. This year my brother Doug, four years younger than myself, who had been playing the baritone for at least four years and was now a freshman, would accompany me.

The grass around the grave stones was trimmed with razor-blade exactness and the American flags adorned the graves of those whose lives had been

118

sacrificed during World War I and World War II. At the time, those were the only wars three generations of recent Americans had experienced. Who had ever heard of Korea, Vietnam or Iraq!

The leaves on the aging maples around the grave sites rustled in the springtime brightness. I lifted the cornet to my lips and played each phrase in front of a flag-covered grave marker. A crowd had gathered to memorialize the not-forgotten heroes. Brother Doug stood tall, on a hillside fifty yards away, in his orange and black school band uniform and repeated each phrase expertly on his shiny baritone. The smooth, mellow notes were like an echo drifting off a soft mountain and spraying the crowd in the valley below with a feeling of togetherness.

More than once I saw someone in the crowd pull out a tissue to wipe away a tear.

And more than once, as I finished a phrase of Taps and heard Doug's echoing notes, I too had a tear in my heart and mentally gave thanks to those whose lives were sacrificed for my benefit. Yet, it wasn't until many decades later that I realized the true sacrifice they had made.

And it wasn't until years later that I realized Doug and I had played Taps the old-fashioned way . . . the way that echoes the lives of the dedicated service men and women throughout America.

CHAPTER TWENTY NINE

Birthdays are wonderful things,
but they make you keep getting older.

When Jane surprised me so overwhelmingly on my 70th birthday on May 23 the previous year, it took me over a year to do the same for her on her 71st. And it was a whopper! Months before her birthday on October 21, 2007, I had arranged, in private, for each of our kids and grand kids to e-mail a message to her relating an experience they had had with Mom/Grandma that would always stick with them to appreciate her in their lives.

I had also arranged to have their messages sent to a good friend and neighbor, Nelson Altenberndt, because if they sent them to our computer, Jane would obviously be certain to see them before I wanted her to. Then when I would hear from Nelson that a message had arrived, I would take my memory stick over and copy them.

After receiving them all, I then copied them on our computer, printed them off when Jane wasn't home and bound them in a plastic binder with the title page reading, *Letters of Love from a Loving Family*, and presented them to her on her birthday. The results where phenomenal. As were the writers! One day shortly after her birthday, Jane and I were at Brenda's and most of her family was present. Brenda began reading them aloud and before she was finished, everyone in the room was in tears. Our family, including the grandchildren, had written such emotional and beautiful memories that have been cherished ever since.

CHAPTER THIRTY

In the rhythm of life we sometimes find ourselves out of tune.
But as long as there are friends to provide the melody,
the music plays on.

The following wraps up our 2007 Christmas Letter sent to friends who didn't already know what was happening in our lives. (We never sent it to those close friends who already knew). More details follow the letter below:

"The Chinese would call it, 'The Year of the Knife.' Jane had her second knee replacement; Lowell had cataract surgery on both eyes and even had to have a toe nail removed. On the upside is that he can probably get 10% off if he ever decides on a pedicure.

We had a wonderful time with good friends in Ft. Myers, FL last December through April and are looking forward to returning on December 18 this year. The sunshine does fit us better than the gloomy, wintry days in Michigan. But we always hope for at least one snow storm before we leave so we can enjoy the beauty of fresh snow on our pine trees.

Jane still enjoys being a volunteer at the Gift Shop at Mid-Michigan Hospital in Midland. She seems to be seeing more and more of our "old" Midland friends there, mostly as patients.

Although not a volunteer, Lowell has been doing some substitute teaching in a communications class Dave has been teaching for Mid-Michigan Community College twice a week. On several occasions Dave has had to be out of town.

This year we have four grandchildren in college; Stacy at Hope College, Kevin at Lawrence Technological University, Ashley, a sophomore at Hope College and Jodi is a freshman at CMU. Wow! How did they grow up so fast?

This fall we enjoyed a cruise down the Columbia and Snake Rivers through Oregon, Washington and Idaho. The scenery reminded us of the song, "America the Beautiful."

We have been very excited this fall with the results of the Boston College football team. At the time of this writing they are second in the nation. Frank Spaziani, defense coordinator, is a friend of ours through marriage to one of our best friends, Laura Heikel, from Midland. Frank has since been promoted to head coach at BC.

From our family to yours, a fun-filled holiday season, and a New Year filled with happiness. Always remember the reason for the season.

CHAPTER THIRTY ONE

Hospitals are wonderful places, but they are full of sick people.

The following was written in the waiting room at Midland Hospital while Jane was undergoing her second knee replacement. She complained about my writing so much about her surgeries, etc., but this was our life as life got older. And writing, for me, was a form of therapy. If I could put my thoughts on paper the paper seemed to soak up my frustrations.

June 25, 2007

A DAY IN THE LIFE OF A CARE-GIVER
(and thankful for it)

It was 4:30 p.m. when the surgeon, Dr. Bortel, approached me in the waiting room. It was a surprise to see him because he had just been there 15 minutes before, talking with others waiting for the same reason as I.

"We have a snag," he informed me, as he sat down opposite me.

My heart sank. It was the second setback. Jane was supposed to have been admitted to surgery at 11:00 a.m. But a phone call at 9:00 a.m. changed that to 12:00 noon. That meant surgery would undoubtedly begin about 2:00 p.m.

We arrived on time and Jane went through the normal admitting procedures, taking about 45 minutes. I left her about 1:30 as she was being wheeled, already in a sleepy state, to the operating room "holding pen." The nurse said the surgery would take about 1.5 hours.

By brilliant mathematical calculations, she would be in recovery by 3:30. By 5:30 she would be awake, although groggy, in her assigned room. Not!

"Our problem is that the air conditioning went out in that area of the hospital," Dr. Bortel stated firmly. "Just when we were ready to begin, I watched

the temperature rise to 75 and the humidity shot up to 90." He went on, "In that humidity, the room and all the equipment in it is no longer sterile."

Jane had already been out for over two hours. "It will take at least a half-to-one-hour to re-sterilize even the trays," he added, "but I think there is another O.R. available and we'll move her there if there is." Fifteen minutes later, a nurse approached me and informed me the move had been accomplished. I thought that was nice of her . . . and of Dr. Bortel. She didn't mention when surgery would commence, however, nor did I have the presence of mind to ask. Dumb me!

Jane hadn't had anything to eat since 7:30 the night before, as per doctor's orders. The upside is that she has wanted to shed a few pounds. This may be a good start.

Still calculating, I figured that if the surgery begins at 5:00, she may not be in her room, able to talk, until 8:30. A long day just got longer!

I kept checking the electronic scheduling board in the room that kept tabs on the status of each patient. When I checked the board at 5:10, it showed that Jane was in surgery. Thank God! It also showed that it had begun at 17:03 (5:03 p.m.).

What bothered me most at this particular time, were signs on the wall that read, "Cell phone use prohibited in Medical Center due to the interference with Patient Equipment." Actually, it wasn't the signs that bothered me. It was the fact that two of the remaining seven of us in the room at that time of day were using cell phones; one for at least 20 minutes. The other was standing in front of one of the signs, situated next to a row of pay phones. She made at least four more calls from her cell. I guess that's why, when I worked in adult education for the Midland Public Schools back in the 1980s, that I helped instigate the Adult Literacy Program in Midland County.

The kind volunteer attendant at the desk had left at 4:30 so there was no one to report this illiterate to.

At 7:35 Dr. Bortel returned to the waiting room. It was easy to find me because I was the only one there. He said that everything went smoothly. There was little bleeding and he fitted her with "whatever" the same size as her other one (her other knee had received the same treatment a year-and-a-half prior). Somehow I hadn't given that a thought. He told me she would be out for a couple hours so I might as well get something to eat. A good idea. My Slim-Fast at 8:00 that morning was wearing a bit slim . . . fast! I had had only a Granola Bar since that time.

I sauntered down to the hospital cafeteria where I knew they had good food. But food was not to be had. They had closed ten minutes earlier. My next option *was a Mexican restaurant nearby. I also debated as to whether to leave the hospital. I had the perfect parking spot, almost in front of the front door. I knew that the spot would be taken when I returned. But the growling in my stomach led me on.*

Having been at this restaurant but once, years ago, I couldn't remember if they served drinks. I was ready for one . . . or two. The smiling waitress, who looked like she had just graduated from eighth grade, took my order. I asked if they served cocktails. "That depends. What would you like?" "Scotch," I replied. "I think so, I'll go ask." If she doesn't know if they have Scotch, then the bartender probably doesn't know how to fix a Rob Roy, I thought.

Before she could leave, I asked, "Do you have Chardonnay wine?" (I thought I should ad the word, "wine" so she would know what I was talking about). Even a bartender can't ruin that. Fortunately they had it and the waitress didn't even have to check to see if they had it.

I also ordered a cup of tortilla soup and a small salad. She brought the soup in a bowl half the size of a kitchen sink. "Is that a cup?" I asked. She replied, smiling, "You ordered a bowl." I mentioned that I never order a bowl when I order something to go with it. (But I might have said "bowl" with the stress of the day still smoldering). Still smiling, she said, "I'll check with the manager to see if I can just charge you for a cup," and she turned away. The soup was delicious, but I didn't want to swim in it. I could only eat about a cup of it with my salad, which was also delicious.

The check came and I was charged for a cup. I left a 25% tip. It must have been the smile.

The second best thing that happened all day was getting back to the hospital to find my old parking spot in front of the front door. The best thing was the surgeon's success with Jane's operation. I thanked him for putting in such a long day. But I didn't tip him 25% for his services. He didn't smile that much.

Jane was still pretty groggy when they wheeled her into her room. She would fall asleep in the middle of a sentence. I would laugh, she would partially wake up and ask what I was laughing about and before I could answer, fall back to sleep. Before I left, she had eaten half a turkey sandwich and some fruit. The other half of the sandwich was delicious. The fruit wasn't bad either.

Another positive for the day was that I finished reading the story of how General MacArthur lost, and then won, the Philippines in WWII with spies, saboteurs, guerrillas and secret missions. And I completed organizing my notes to begin writing the second volume of this autobiography.

Sorry to take so long to tell you that Jane is in a lot of pain, which is expected and she has some nausea. But is doing fine otherwise. Her therapy begins on Wednesday and will undoubtedly be coming home on Thursday. But if I didn't write like this while under stress, I would end up in the hospital . . . only it would be a mental one. Besides, writers write! (I think that's right. I read that once).

CHAPTER THIRTY TWO

Don't be afraid to lose a battle if it helps you win the war.

2007 held another very important event in our lives also. A couple years previous, Shelly Brady, daughter of our very good friend, Phyllis Miller, gave to her step-dad, Mel, some information from the Internet. Mel, a World War II veteran, handed it to me one day and said, "Why don't you see what you can do with this?"

It was information regarding an organization called "Honor Flight," an organization that was, as funding allowed, flying World War II veterans to Washington, D.C. to see the relatively new WWII Memorial.

I gave the material to the Midland Daily News, thinking they would jump at the chance to be a part of this with The Dow Chemical Company. Nothing happened for nearly a year and I, being busy with senior citizen stuff, i.e. travel, care-giving, etc., etc., (to say nothing about a bad memory) forgot about it. I had even forgotten the Website where the information came from.

Finally, a year later, I called Shelly, who is gifted with a better (and younger) memory, told me where to find the information. Then I contacted Phyllis and Mel's other daughter/stepdaughter who worked for the vice president of public relations at Dow as to whom to contact. She knew immediately. This time I followed through and on November 7, 2007, a chartered plane loaded with World War II veterans and retirees of Dow took off for Washington, D.C. and their Memorial. Several of the veterans were written up in my book.

To my good fortune, I was invited to go along!

The following I wrote upon returning from that momentous trip and e-mailed it to family and close friends:

Wow! Can't believe that yesterday I flew over 1,000 miles (round trip), did all I did, saw all I saw, and still slept in my own bed last night. Will try to give a quick run-down, but you might as well get another cup of coffee. It will help relieve the boredom.

When I, and many others, arrived at the local airport (MBS) about 5:00 a.m. yesterday (Thurs.), there must have been a dozen or more Dow employees and volunteers in the parking lot to show us where to park, and a shuttle bus to take us to the terminal. As we arrived at the terminal, there were dozens more inside, waving American flags, holding a large banner and applauding.

While I knew the kudos was for the WWII vets, I was still choked up.

Dow served everyone a Continental breakfast upstairs in the Sky Room and handed out packets of information that had been given to the press. Included were excerpts of six veterans from my book Dow had asked me to write for the cause.

Each vet also received a baseball cap with the Dow diamond and the words "WWII Veteran." Plus, each got a disposable camera and a sweatshirt that reads, "If you can read this, thank a teacher. If you can read this in English, thank a veteran." Really cool!

While the veterans (and attendants who helped those in wheel chairs) loaded onto the chartered plane, I had the distinct pleasure of flying in Dow's corporate jet. It was full, with just ten of us. Two were reporters from Midland and Saginaw, three were former top officials of Dow (also WWII veterans), a Dow V.P. and the rest were current Dow personnel involved in the program from the public relations department. Then there was me. I was the only odd ball in the group, but didn't mind. The others really made me feel welcome.

Wow again! That sleek little bird was smooth as silk in the air. Didn't even know when we left the ground. We flew at 40,000 feet at nearly 500 mph. Took us only an hour and fifteen minutes to D.C.

The inside wasn't bad either. Leather seats that would fold into a bed and plenty of room to move around.

Because private planes aren't allowed to land at Ronald Regan Airport in D.C., we had to land in Manassas, Virginia, about a half-hour away (an hour away, due to traffic, that evening when we returned at 5:30). For the history buffs, Manassas is known for the Battle of Bull Run.

We met up with the troops at Regan and loaded onto busses for the tour. We covered the WWII War Memorial, Arlington cemetery, tomb of the Unknown Soldier, Vietnam Memorial and the Korean Memorial. Plus we saw the Lincoln and Washington monuments and the Capitol.

The WWII War Memorial was inspiring as well as awesome. I was given the responsibility of carrying a folded American flag in a see-through plastic case. The flag came from the casket of a veteran who was scheduled for the trip, but died a few weeks ago. It was to be displayed at the memorial site with a framed picture of the deceased. Dow had a picture taken of it for the family.

But getting the flag there was a surprise for me. As we got off the busses (three of them), I was asked to hand the flag to one of the veterans in a wheel chair and push him to the site through a path made by the other veterans and Dow employees. People waved small American flags and many of the vets removed their hats and saluted . . . and cried. Good grief!! My stomach was in my throat! Then there were TV cameras in our faces and reporters snapping pictures. I nearly lost it. My good friend, Mel, 85, in the wheel chair did. (He's from our church). He cried like a baby as did many of the other veterans. Something the TV news channels love to focus on. I consoled him best I could from behind him, trying to keep my own emotions in check. That's like trying to fry two hamburgers at once; one rare and one well done . . . in the same pan.

It was probably 50 yards from the busses to the memorial but ol' Mel and I made it. Me, with still a lump in my throat that went all the way to my toes.

Senator Bob Dole showed up at the memorial. He saw the lst Infantry Division insignia on my cap and asked if I had been stationed at Ft. Riley, Kansas. (He's from Kansas). I said I was for six months back in the 50s. Then I had my picture taken with him. Yup, me and Bobby are real close. You can tell that by the way he appears to be avoiding me in the picture.

We had a hot, catered lunch in a large tent near the WWII Memorial. It was very good too. Good thing the tent had sides on it as it was becoming quite cool. More politicians showed up after lunch. (Is next year election year? Yup, I think it is). Anyway, Congressman Dave Camp and Senator Stabenow showed up with a pep talk to a group of sleepy veterans.

*Most of the memorials are fairly close together. On my own, I visited the Vietnam Wall. Three times guys wearing Vietnam badges on their jackets came up to me, shook my hand and said, "Welcome home." Not sure what they meant by that. I didn't plan on staying even overnight. But the insignia on my cap told them I had been in the 1*st* Infantry Division. One guy saw my cap and yelled, "Yeah, the Big Red One." I just gave him the thumbs up.*

The afternoon was spent visiting the other memorials and monuments, and about 5:30 the busses left for the airport. We would have left at 5:00, but just as we were about to pull out, Senator Carl Levin stepped on our bus for a ten-minute spiel. We had three busses, so that meant a full half-hour delay. That's the advantage of chartering your own plane . . . or taking someone else's private jet. It doesn't matter what time you get there.

Well, I made the six o'clock news last night, according to Mom/ Grandma, on the local CBS channel. At the WWII Memorial I had two TV interviews and one for a newspaper. We were told there will be something on Good Morning America tomorrow (Friday) morning on ABC. Mom/Grandma says she will be getting me a new pillow because my head won't fit the one I already have. Yeah, it's tough to stay humble.

Landing at MBS was still another celebration. Four hundred people must have been waiting, waving American flags, as the veterans passed through the crowd as it parted for them. Knowing the crowd wasn't waiting for me, I trailed somewhat behind. A high school band from Saginaw, in full uniform, played the marches of the four branches of the military. There was that lump in my throat again. I saw a soldier, of military age, wearing an army uniform. On impulse, I saluted.

I got home at 10:00 p.m. It would have been sooner, but I couldn't find my car in the parking lot. It was dark when I parked it in the morning and dark when I tried to find it last night. Mom/Grandma and I talked for another two hours as I unwound from the humbling experience.

Having made the suggestion to Dow PR a year ago, it has finally become a reality. I should have gone into politics. It's so much fun spending someone else's money. And I know the money Dow spent had to have been in six figures. But what a wonderful thing they have done. It was a terrific staff that put it together and made it work. Most of the WWII veterans would never have seen their monument had it not been for Dow. I surely hope other companies will emulate Dow's effort. As for my friend, Mel; I talked with his wife a few minutes ago and she said he hasn't felt as good in two weeks as he does this morning.

Six of the veterans on the trip had been written up in my book in 2004, and Dow asked me to write a synopsis of their experiences which they included in the PR packet going to the press.

Another plus was that Dow Public Relations purchased from me, 120 copies of Silent Heroes. *They gave a copy to each veteran at the end of the trip. I had previously endorsed the books with "Thank you!" and signed my name. Because of the quantity, I reduced the price enough so that I contributed $1100 to the cause. After the trip, I received phone calls from veterans and families, thanking me for not only writing the book, but for following through with the whole idea to Dow. Because of the publicity, I sold several more books.*

Well, either your coffee is cold or you've fallen asleep by now, so won't keep you any longer. Thanks for your interest and concerns.

Love 'n stuff,

Dad/Gramps

One of the letters of gratitude came from the daughter of one of the veterans in my book and also whom we got to know when Jane was going through her treatment for breast cancer. Garlene Glanze worked at the Midland Community Cancer Services. In part, her letter read:

Dear Lowell,

Thank you so much for all that you did to promote the WWII vet's trip to Washington, D.C. I know you are very much aware of how much it meant to each one of those guys. I overheard one of them say that he would remember it for the rest of his life. You are a very special person and I am thrilled to be able to say I know you!

Garlene Glanz

As the result (I think) of all that hoopla, I was invited to speak at a special veteran's day program at Dow on Veteran's Day that year. It was such an honor. I have written hundreds of speeches over the years, some taking weeks to write and to polish. But the one I delivered that day took probably ten minutes, and there was little to polish. I liked it from the moment it was put on paper. Following is that speech:

November 12, 2007
The Dow Chemical Company

WE CAN SEE YOU NOW

What a thrill is for me to stand here and to address such a distinguished audience. Thank you so much, Leona, for inviting me.

In the introduction to the book, Silent Heroes, I implied that it was the gray hairs in Washington who made the decisions regarding the war but that it was the men in their late teens and early 20s who won it.

As I look out over this audience today, I can see that it was the gray hairs here who <u>really</u> won it.

I was nine years old when the atom bombs were dropped on Japan. But one of the years preceding that, I remember lying on the floor of my parent's living room with my coloring book and crayons. As I lay there coloring, I was

133

also listening to my parents, discussing with their friends, how badly things were going for us in Europe and in the South Pacific.

I don't know if it was anger or frustration, but I had to leave the room. Even at that age, I had had enough of this bad news. I really didn't know what was going on, but they were talking about men I didn't know and would most likely never meet. I'm so glad history has changed that.

I do remember the white cloth banners with the blue stars on them, hanging in the window of a lot of houses in my home town. That indicated that a young man from that home was serving in the war. Sometimes there was more than one blue star on the banner. And sometimes there was a gold star on the banner, indicating that someone from that home had made the supreme sacrifice. There were a lot of both colors on those banners as I recall.

But that didn't seem to mean a whole lot to me at the time. Those stars simply meant something to those in those homes as far as I was concerned. I don't remember even seeing the faces, and many of them my parents hadn't either.

My wife and I have been fortunate to be able to travel a great deal and we have seen some of those scarred buildings in Germany, and the bullet holes that still exist on some buildings in Budapest. But these were merely symbols of a time gone by. We didn't see the faces of the men who put them there.

We have stood on the ground where Hitler reviewed his men and war machines in Nuremburg, making his people believe he had the best and the most to win his war. But again, that was a time gone by and we didn't see the faces behind the plot, nor those of the plotters.

As a 20-year-old, I once stood on a bridge in Hiroshima, looking out over the wasteland of what was called the Atomic Desert. And that wasteland was caused by an atomic bomb that killed over 100,000 people. It has been argued, even by the Japanese in later years, that the bomb saved <u>many</u> times that many. But we never saw the faces of those who made the decision to drop that bomb, nor those who carried out the orders . . . at least, not until much later. And that was in the news media.

I know for a fact, that many of you were in training to head for the Japanese homeland and that some of you were already on your way for that invasion when the bomb was dropped. I know at least one Marine here who was, and before he boarded the ship to take him there, he wrote his parents telling them to get ready to collect his life insurance. That's how sure he was of never coming back.

But for most of us, we never saw your battle-weary faces or felt the feelings that many of you have felt. And many of you have never, to this day, expressed those feelings. That's why, in my book, I called you silent heroes.

At this time I would like to have our veterans stand and remain standing . . . Gentlemen, WE CAN SEE YOU NOW. Thank you for what you did for us and for our great country . . . may God continue to bless you all. (Salute)

The applause was heart-warming.

The person who worked out most of the WWII expedition plans to the War Memorial in Washington, D.C. was a nice lady, Jennifer Heronema, who worked in Dow's public relations department. Unfortunately, two years later, due to the economy, she was down-sized out of a job. She then established her own PR company in Midland.

When I heard this, I e-mailed her a note stating what a valued employee Dow had lost and wished her well in her new venture.

In response she wrote:

> *Lowell, Thanks for the sweet note. Hands down, Dow Honor Flight was the most rewarding project of my career. I'm so glad that you and I found each other and that we were able to make your request a reality. I hope to cross paths with you one of these days. Until then, take care! Jen*

Earlier I had told her that it was ironic that her last name began with the word, "Hero." She was truly a hero to over 200 WWII veterans, and a hero to me for making my dream a reality.

CHAPTER THIRTY THREE

On becoming older: Your kids are becoming you . . . and they're OK,
but your grandkids are perfect.

2007, for the most part, was a very good year for Jane and me. But
Kevin, now in his senior year at Lawrence Tech University, was becoming
discouraged . . . not so much from his studies, it just seemed to him that
the goal of a B.S. degree was still far away. (We learned this from Brenda
who asked me to e-mail him and try to pep him up a bit). I sent him the
following letter:

May 12, 2007

Hi Kev,

   As I was falling asleep last night I was thinking of you and where
you are in your life, and couldn't help but remember where I was and
some of my thoughts I had at that stage in mine. (I never told him his
mother had asked me to write him to help spur him on. Brenda
knew he was getting discouraged).
   If I recall, I was somewhat discouraged. The target (graduation) was
in sight but it still seemed so far away. I just wanted to get there and get
on with my life! You already have more going for you than most have at
your stage; tuition reimbursements and a job offer with good pay. Wow!
Good for you!
   You have had a really long grind, Kev, with a full load each semester,
then summer school every summer. I have to admire your ambition and
your energy to complete the task. You have really kept at it and I know
you will always be doing your utmost to reach your goals. And when/

if your goals change, you will adapt to whatever it takes to accomplish them.

Whenever I got discouraged, and I did at times, I tried to remember that that was natural at different points in life. It didn't make the discouragement any easier, but it reminded me that I was human. And that I wouldn't want to be anything else.

I also remembered the story of the duck. When we see a duck sailing along the surface of the water, smooth and carefree as can be, just remember that under the surface he is paddling like hell! It's that stamina and energy that's expended under the surface that gets him where he wants to go.

OK, enough Grandpa philosophy. You probably aren't anything like I described myself when I was 21. However, if you are, just remember the duck.

> *With much love,*
> *Grandpa*

Kevin always had a response to our letters and sometimes his gratitude was so generous that it would bring a tear from the soft tissue. The following, in part, was one of them:

Grandpa, I can't thank you enough for your words of wisdom! I read your e-mail earlier today while I was waiting for my physics tutor. You are more than inspirational! I love you! You put a smile on my face and your words gave me the ambition I needed to get through the day and my frustrations with physics.

For instance, I submitted both of my physics assignments on-line and received 100% on both of them. (I did have help from a tutor, but that was academic help). I believe your words truly helped me on a much higher level than just academics!

Kevin would do well in the public relations field . . . even though this was private.

Senator Bob Dole and I (Mel Miller in foreground)

Dow's Corporate Jet

CHAPTER THIRTY FOUR

Out of the mouth of babes!

I have received many kind letters, both e-mail and U.S. Mail. Many are posted in this book. Probably one of the most endearing came from daughter, Brenda, on March 26, 2008. It was a P.S. attached to another topic and read:

Dad, your writing ability is truly inspirational for my entire family. I think it's great that two of my three children look to you for inspiration!! Jennifer is very proud of herself (which I credit to you) for having the gift of writing. She has so much to tell you when she sees you again. Her writing just keeps on giving.

Her language arts teacher is helping her with projects and with her grammar, spelling, etc. Not only are you Jen's hero but also mine. Could that be why I want my mommy and daddy when I don't feel good? lol Anyways, here's to you dad, you're great! Kisses to Mom. She's great too!!

WOW! That's where her kids get it.

CHAPTER THIRTY FIVE

Writing is not for the weak-hearted.

In the spring of 2008 I entered a writing contest with the Gulf Coast Writer's Association in the non-fiction genre. While it didn't win any kind of a prize, it helped me put together a piece that conveyed a wonderful fifty years of being married to the former Jane Lapworth. It went like this:

HAPPY ANNIVERSARY, SWEETHEART

Jane was a gorgeous bride. Whenever I look at our wedding pictures even today I think, *Little wonder I fell in love with this delightful lady.*

The wedding was held at the local Methodist Church. More than once people who attended told us there was something "special" about our wedding. Whatever it was, it has lasted for over five decades. If anything made it special it was beautiful Jane, with whom I have been madly in love with ever since. OK, maybe not madly . . . passionately would be more appropriate.

The wedding reception was held at the church for close friends and relatives and later at Jane's parent's home for out-of-town guests.

My old '53 Chevrolet was parked in Jane's neighbor's garage to avoid anyone decorating it and adding the traditional (at the time) tin cans tied to the rear bumper to draw attention to the newly-weds as they drove through town.

Just prior to the wedding, I let out the information to a relative whom I knew would tell all, if he knew all, the location of our car. And right on schedule, the car was decorated with the tin cans and the "Just Married" signs painted on the windows with a harmless, washable paint.

At the given time, younger brother, Doug, drove up to Jane's front door with Dad's brand new 1958 Chevrolet. Doug jumped out, Jane and I got in and drove off for our honeymoon. Dad had offered us his new car for the trip, unknown to anyone but my parents and brother.

My parents had the "pleasure" of driving our decorated car down our small town Main Street to their home. They were kind enough to clean it up but didn't give a thought to taking a picture of it. Jane and I never did know what we could have driven off in.

Earlier, Jane and I had decided where we would spend our first night together. It was in a motel only twenty miles from home. I was the first to awaken the next morning. When I saw the sun coming in the window, I nudged Jane, saying it was time to head up the road.

It wasn't until we had both showered and dressed that we realized it was 3:00 a.m. The "sun" I had seen coming in the window was a yellowish insect repellent light outside our door.

We undressed and went back to bed.

As a surprise for Jane, I had ordered a dozen red roses delivered to our room for my new bride. Carrying the roses everywhere we went during our honeymoon, no one would guess we were newlyweds.

When we returned home Jane told her mother about the roses. Her response was, "Isn't that nice? Now on your anniversaries he can give you an additional rose to represent each year of your marriage."

That's what I had had in mind, but because my mother-in-law had suggested it, the idea suffered a rapid death. In retrospect, it was good it happened that way for more than one reason. What would we do today with over fifty roses in the house each year?

Economically, in 1958 the cost of a dozen roses was $3. Today each rose can cost that much. That's $150 for something that would be thrown out in just a few days. Thank you, Mother.

Jane's mother was good at suffocating ideas. During rehearsal the night before the wedding her ideas became overwhelming for this twenty-two year old. I felt my life was out of control. When I dropped Jane off at her house following rehearsal, I suggested we call the whole thing off and elope. Her father had already offered us $500 to do so, and even in 1958 that would have saved him a bundle. Her mother had vetoed that idea also. Jane assured me that since her mother was picking up the tab, she had the privilege of being in control. Somehow that vaguely made sense to me but I assured her that her mother would not run the rest of our lives. As it turned out, my mother-in-law was one of the best parts of our marriage.

Thanks to the encouragement of Jane over the past fifty years, I have been successful in teaching and in administration in public schools, in college administration, a national seminar leader in continuing and adult education, plus a sideline of other achievements. One of which was radio broadcasting.

In the early 1990s I had my own daily radio program on our small town local radio station. It was called, "Thomas Tidbits for Today." It was only two to three minutes each day, but the owner pretty much gave me free reign over its contents.

On August 16, 1993, I broadcast the following:

They had known each other since fourth grade, although they had never been sweethearts until many years later, following their graduation from high school, his military stint, and she, a senior in college.

At 22 he realized she was the most beautiful, wonderful person he had ever known. They were married, and within the next five years produced two of the most delightful children the world would ever know.

This wonderful, witty woman saw him through his college years by bringing home the pay check, thus meeting the bills.

Whenever he disagreed with her she found a diplomatic way to work things out—and eventually it always worked out to the advantage of both.

He placed her on a pedestal as she continued working hard to support their ideas, their dreams and their ambitions, and she enhanced his love for her through so many unselfish and often unsaid ways.

She laughed with him and laughed at him, and she would even laugh when she heard his corny jokes for the 20th time.

When times were tough, she was there to see him through them. When times were on a high, she was there to ride the wave with him.

This lady could read him like a book, and more often than not, she served his every need before he knew he needed anything.

When he was <u>discouraged</u> she saw to it that he could <u>begin</u> that word with an 'en.' When he was down, she let him know in her own inimitable, loving way, that he was, certainly, not out.

When he hurt, she hurt. And sometimes, when her own aches and pains became nearly unbearable, she still put him first.

I know that beautiful, wonderful and witty woman well. You see, she became by bride . . . 35 years ago . . . today.

Happy anniversary, sweetheart.

That's Thomas Tidbits for today. I'm Lowell Thomas, saying . . . so long until tomorrow.

(That final sentence I plagiarized from my namesake. For fifty years he ended his news broadcasts with the same sentence. But only members of my generation would know that).

Today, more than fifteen years after that broadcast and fifty years after that "special" wedding, that true love still exists.

And fifty times I have had the privilege of saying, "Happy anniversary, sweetheart." Sometimes I even buy her a rose.

I also submitted it to the book publisher that puts out the books "Chicken Soup for the Soul" with no result. But I still like it and read it to the people at our winter home in Ft. Myers, Florida the day they were commerating those celebrating their 50th anniversary. There were seven couples in all. I even choked in a couple places in the reading because it was so close to my heart.

On August 16, 2008, something else rang close to our hearts as well . . . Jane and I had been married for fifty years! We had been planning for the event for months, which included a pig roast in the yard near the lake, 88 guests and members of our family attended. Among the guests were former high school and college friends, participants in our wedding and friends and neighbors from Midland and around the lake. Jane even wore the veil she had worn in our wedding a half-century earlier.

David and son-in-law Jerry Bouchey, did most of the roasting and attending to the large, rented grill most of the night before. It turned out succulent! Along with all the food brought by others, we gave quantities to our guests and family to take home and we had leftovers for days.

This was just the conclusion of the activities, however. A main event was planned by me a year in advance. I made the right connections during that time and at about 6:30 a.m., Jane and I, along with our Hope United

Methodist minister, Pat Poag, lifted from the ground near the Midland Fair Grounds in a hot air balloon.

All of us managed to keep it a secret from Jane until just a few days prior to our anniversary. Jane was becoming so stressed that the pig roast would turn out right, that she was becoming very . . . well, GRUMPY!! To give her something different to think about, just a few days before the event, I broke down and told her what I had been planning for nearly a year. Somehow her attitude changed as she realized I too had some original thoughts for our celebration. She became the same plain Jane I had known for over a half-century.

The balloon and basket glided two hundred or more feet above the trees and highways in this early hour, carrying our pilot, our pastor and Jane and I silently along about a ten mile stretch. The experience reminded Jane and I of gliding silently along the waters of many lakes in our Sunfish sailboat many years before. Only the rush of the wind was audible.

The reason for our pastor accompanying us was to have a "mock" wedding, him reading the scripture and praying and Jane and I recited our vows which we had both written beforehand.

Jane read hers first. Or at least, I thought she was going to read them. She fooled me and had memorized her lines, reciting from memory. When she finished, I said, "You cheated!" Just then, the pilot triggered the gases in the basket, forcing the balloon to lift higher above the trees. It made a horrendous noise!

I waited the few seconds for the noise to stop, then began again. I repeated, "You cheated." Chuckling, I added, "I thought you were going to <u>read</u> your lines, but you memorized them and gave them by heart. I will now <u>read</u> you my message." I couldn't help but think what the pilot and Pastor Pat thought I was going to say after they heard the first two words and had to wait a moment as to what was coming next. I'm certain they both had a sigh of relief.

Our messages were brief and relayed some of what the past fifty years had brought us and how much our love had meant during that time.

August 16, 1958

Celebrating our 50th Wedding Anniversary.

From the hot air balloon

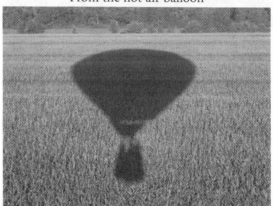

Me and my shadow.

Hot air balloon, a perfect landing.

CHAPTER THIRTY SIX

Traveling is educational. That's why Jane and I
are among the smartest people in the world.

In early fall of 2008, Jane and I had a wonderful ten-day cruise to, and partly through, the Panama Canal. With us were equally wonderful friends, Dave and Jan Weissenborn from Grayling, MI and Curt and Peggy Young from Matteson, IL. As always, I took along my trusty lap top computer and recorded it for history. I was even paid for it by the *Midland Daily News* as I submitted it in a several-part story. And that was how it was published. Below is the content of those stories:

Cruising With a Princess . . . PART 1

The 92,000 ton cruise ship, *Coral Princess,* glided effortlessly through the Atlantic Ocean and into the Caribbean Sea as it rounded the south-eastern end of Cuba.

Hours earlier, the ship had left Ft. Lauderdale in bright sunshine for which Florida is famous. Now the only lights on shore were those shining from the Communist country indicating, in the inky darkness, the rocky shoreline.

This trip had been a work in progress for nearly a year and the logistics had been worked out by our travel agent in Ft. Myers, Florida where we spend the worst part of the Michigan winters.

There is nothing like traveling with good friends, and this time we were with our frequent traveling companions, Dave and Jan Weissenborn. Dave and Jan were both teachers in Bullock Creek and now live on the Manistee River in Grayling. Dave was also the chairman of the board of Members First Credit Union (formerly Teacher's Credit Union). Included this time were Curt and Peggy Young, members of Plantation Estates where we spend the winters in Ft. Myers. Curt is a retired executive from IBM in Chicago and Peggy worked in a medical facility near Chicago. Jane and I have always been blessed with great friends.

Aruba

After two full days and a night of cruising the low to moderate waves, of first the Atlantic, then the Caribbean, the *Coral Princess* docked on the island of Aruba, just off the east coast of Columbia, South America. Like all cities in the tropics, the streets were lined with palm trees. Early on, we had decided to opt for roaming the streets instead of signing up for one of the many tours of the island. We were only going to be here a few hours.

Not taking a tour might have been a mistake. The streets just off the pier were crammed full of small shops with the natives hawking their souvenir wares. The really good stores, because it was Sunday, were closed. I thought of the hundreds (there were nearly 2,000 passengers on our ship) of potential customers these businesses passed up because they didn't want to open on a Sunday.

But we had missed some opportunities too by not signing up for a tour of the island.

Cartagena (Cart-a-hain-ya), Columbia

Leaving Aruba at 2:00 p.m., we sailed north and west to arrive at Cartagena around 10:00 a.m. the following day. This time we decided to take a tour of the city by one of the local mini-bus drivers.

With 20 people aboard, and with Mary, a local lady, but with not a whole lot of English speaking ability, we headed into the city from the pier. Little did we know this would be a mistake as well.

"We will walk the wall," Mary said. Cartagena has a concrete wall that was built around the city hundreds of years ago, and for 200 years it was the city's fortress, keeping pirates at bay.

We parked near the wall, but first Mary led the group down a street away from the wall and into the metropolis. She also led us into a jewelry store where people browsed at will and were sold items they didn't need or want. Some of us didn't come on this trip to purchase jewelry and on our way out of the store, there was Mary accepting money from whom we thought to be the store owner. She apparently got paid for bringing the tourists to the store.

But before that happened, we learned that Mary's leadership was even worse than her English. Restless, many of us left the store and walked down the street. Some even broke off into smaller groups and ventured in other directions. Mary was nowhere to be seen. Eventually she appeared and tried to gather her chicks as would a mother hen, but she couldn't find all of them. So she would dart off in another direction, leaving the rest of us stranded, not knowing where we were or where we could find the bus.

We walked in the direction she had last pointed and soon saw our bus driver who led us to his vehicle. It was apparent, however, that he was also miffed at the confusion caused by Mary, who never told us where or when to meet if we got split up. The *Coral Princess,* with its nearly 2000 passengers and 900 crew members was better organized than Mary with her flock of twenty.

Eventually it all came together, but by then there was no time to walk the wall and we had to head back to the ship. Most of us felt that Mary had already received her tip and most of us gave her nothing at the end of the journey.

Limon (Le-moan), Costa Rica

An early morning rain greeted us in Limon, and everyone hoped that was the only rain we would receive that day because all of us were to be out in the weather most of the day. Curt and I signed up for the rigorous flight through the jungle in a harness on a cable. In Limoneze talk it is called a "Zip Line."

Dave, Jan, Peggy and Jane opted for the Rain Forest Aerial Tram. A two-hour bus ride took them to the edge of a rain forest where they transferred to a smaller bus.

Being on the floor of the rain forest, they walked along while the guide pointed out various plants, flowers and insects, including spiders the size of a 50-cent piece. Eventually they boarded a six-passenger tram, much like a miniature cable car, attached to a cable that took them through the center of the rain forest, approximately ten to sixty feet in the air. All the while their guide, in a hushed voice, pointed out interesting scenes below, above and around them in the forest. The excursion ended with lunch and, of course, a tour of the local gift ship.

The tram passed through and over areas growing bananas and pineapple. (Costa Rica is number two in the world for exporting bananas).

While the others in our entourage thought they were having an unusual experience, it was nothing to what Curt and I experienced.

First, twenty of us from the *Coral Princess* who had the same adventurous frame of mind, boarded a mini-bus at the pier and headed somewhere into another rain forest an hour distant. We had no idea where we were going, but the scenery was gorgeous. We passed various species of palms, tropical flowers and bushes and even encountered a couple snail-like-moving sloths. The bus driver would stop each time so people could observe and take pictures. Jane had our only camera so all I could do was put them in my memory . . . and that's not a particularly good thing because neither is the memory. But my buddy, Curt, had a digital camera and later e-mailed the pictures to me.

The roads in Costa Rica must resemble those in the U.S. during the 1930's . . . or 40's. Few roads were paved and those that were, were full of pot holes. For awhile we thought we were back in Michigan . . . except for the palm trees.

But our driver, Pedro, who was familiar with the roads, masterfully avoided the rough spots and had to know he saved his passengers many times while avoiding those spots, pedestrians, other traffic and the deep ditches on either side. Even when the speed limit was 35mph, he knew the safe speed was 20mph. Actually, most of the time the speed limit wasn't even posted. You are on your own. At the end of the trip I awarded Pedro, out of gratitude, a bigger tip than I did our step-on guide.

When our bus full of happy wanderers arrived at the launch point, we were fitted with a harness and a pair of leather gloves and given instructions on how to maneuver oneself over the trees that were sometimes 100 feet or more above the floor of the rain forest. We also received a crash helmet. I didn't like the sound of that, but perhaps the attendants defined the word "crash" differently than I.

If the harness was not attached properly, it could result in one of two things: 1) your body would be air-lifted from the floor of the rain forest by helicopter, or 2) for the men, it meant singing soprano in the church choir. (Five days after arriving back in Ft. Myers, the local newspaper carried a story about a Texas woman, doing the zip line in Honduras, fell sixty-five feet to her death when her harness apparently broke).

Before we boarded the bus for our journey into the wild, someone in our group, I think it was Jan, reminded me that I was already half of a Tarzan team because I was married to Jane. So twice on the nine times we sped over the trees on the man-made cable, I gave out a Tarzan call. Neither time did anyone in our group of twenty or so, give any response (I don't think even Jane would have been proud of me) so I didn't Tarzan call anymore.

But what a rush! An attendant would attach our harness to the cable, tell us to sit down, and before our bottom end reached the platform in a sitting position, gravity already had its pull and we were off to the next platform, some several hundred feet away. The platforms were made of steel grating and attached to huge mahogany trees, some of which were over a hundred feet tall.

"No need to panic," the attendant said, smiling. I didn't like his attitude. It was a smooth ride, but when one looked down, one suddenly realized that what one was looking down at was not the green carpet of the rain forest floor . . . it was the tops of trees. It was panic time!

Sailing over the tops of other trees and our feet sometimes going through the leaves of others at 25 mph, there was no time to panic. And on the next platform there was always an attendant to help us glide in safely. There we would wait until ten or twelve others were congregated, then off we would go once again, one at a time, on to the next platform.

After a couple hours of this we ended up back at the station from which we had launched. Rain threatened during the afternoon, but it didn't happen. The humidity, however, was something else. It was close to 100%.

We knew the others would be back later so Curt and I shopped the shops at the end of the pier. It looked like a huge flea market. Much to our surprise, one of the curio shops was run by members of a local Indian tribe. It wasn't the Indian tribe itself that caught our attention, but the way they were dressed . . . or not. The men wore nothing but loin cloths and the women wore nothing from the waist up . . . not that we noticed all that much, but by the time we were back at the ship I could not remember what they had been selling.

NEXT: The Panama Canal, Jamaica and the Bra Incident

Cruising With a Princess . . . Part II

The Panama Canal

The major destination for the cruise was the Panama Canal. What a marvel of engineering which has been in operation for nearly 100 years, connecting the Atlantic and Pacific Oceans. The *Coral Princess* went through only three of the locks and anchored in Gatun (Ga-toon) Lake, the largest man-made lake in the world. Actually, it is the water in the lake, fed by the rain forests, that is used to operate the levels of the canals. To use salt water from the ocean would rapidly corrode the mechanisms operating the locks.

Continuing our education, we learned that the project was first launched in the minds of men in 1534 by Charles I of Spain, but the canal was not completed until August 1914, primarily by the United States, at a cost of $387 million dollars. In today's dollars it would be just over seven billion dollars.

What a thrill it was to experience a world phenomenon that we first learned about in elementary school. The pictures we had seen in the textbooks sixty years ago suddenly came to life.

As the water levels changed between the locks, powerful engines on either side of the canal and attached by steel cables, pulled the ships into the next lock. These engines were called "mules."

For the *Coral Princess* to traverse the fifty miles through the locks, it would have cost the Princess Cruise Lines around $245,600, a fee levied on net tonnage. We were never told how much it cost to travel just the three locks and into the lake.

But we did learn the average toll for ocean-going commercial vessels is around $35,000 for the trip. I did wonder if the war ships that travel the canal were charged the fee during war time when America controlled the canal.

After anchoring in Lake Gatun, tenders from the ship were lowered, and those who had signed for the land tour, were transported to another pier, loaded into busses, then to a train which took us all the way to the Pacific Ocean and back to the busses which transported us once again to the pier where we boarded the tenders for the return trip to the ship. It was a long day, and the only time most of us will ever see the Atlantic and Pacific Oceans in one day without ever stepping on an airplane.

Ocho (O-cho) Rios, Jamaica

Gentle breezes danced across our skin while the warm sun was painting a dazzling canvas of blue-green mountains, white sand and turquoise waters. That was our introduction to Jamaica as we easily cruised the shoreline at 6:00 a.m. when I was taking my daily walk on deck seven. I tried to keep my calorie output at least even to the calorie intake by walking my usual 2-3 miles per day. It wasn't working.

A pleasant part of arriving in Jamaica was hearing the sound of steel drums being played by the natives, and on the sidewalks singing the songs of the islands. Of course they want you to contribute to the boxes placed in front of them for their efforts and/or talents. And sometimes you want to contribute and ask them to develop their talents. I don't have the greatest ear for music, even though I used to play trumpet, but I do know when someone is off-key. And the trademark for the island was the saying, "No problem, mon." I think the natives would use this phrase even if there *was* a problem.

Never before, not even on other cruises, had we encountered such a wonderful variety of delicious food. It didn't matter if we were in the formal dining room or the informal cafeteria or one of the numerous snack bars on the ship. It would have been a sin not to try them all. After all, we had paid for it, hadn't we? But I really blame my mother. How many times, while growing up, had I heard the lecture about cleaning my plate because of all the starving kids in China? Somehow I never grasped the correlation. Mother should have simply lectured about how much food one puts on one's plate.

The Bra Incident

An interesting thing happened after dinner one night. Jane entered our stateroom first, went to open the drapes that led to our balcony, and exclaimed, "Come here and look!" I did as I was told (that's just my nature whenever Jane beckons).

I looked where she was pointing and was stunned at the sight. At first I thought it might have been a cockroach or some such intrusive thing, but I was looking down at someone's bra on the floor between the end of the sofa and the wall separating the living area from the balcony. Jane knew it wasn't hers and I knew it wasn't hers, so we paged our cabin steward, David. He was the only one who didn't know it wasn't hers, despite it being several sizes smaller than Jane's.

Poor David was a most congenial, hard working young man from the Philippines. He was more stunned than I and when Jane told him the bra was not hers, he bravely picked it up, and without a word, left the cabin. I'm certain that if one looked closely one could see the blush under his dark Filipino skin. He was truly embarrassed.

Not letting it rest, Jane called David's boss, the ship's hotel manager, and asked him who and how someone could use our stateroom while it was assigned to us. Francisco, from Portugal, a true public relations person, assured us he would get to the bottom (or top) of the situation.

The next day Francisco stopped by to say he thought the puzzle was solved. He explained that David thought the bra belonged to Jane so he didn't pick it up . . . no more than he would pick up a pair of dirty socks lying on the floor. We believed him and the next day, after coming back from a land tour, there was a bucket of ice with a bottle of champagne and a tray of chocolate covered strawberries in our room. There was also a note from Francisco, apologizing for any inconvenience or embarrassment the incident had caused. What a nice guy!

This bra incident also taught us how very computerized the ship was. Francisco explained to us that whenever anyone inserted the card-key, much like hotels/motels now use, it leaves an imprint on a computer. The computer tells, on a print-out, the time of day the room was opened and whose card was used.

We were told that besides us, only the cabin steward (David), himself (Francisco), the ship's electrician and plumber can access our room, and the time is recorded as to when each one entered. The print-out showed only that David, Jane and I had entered the room over the past three days, and the time of day we had entered. We apologized to David for his embarrassment and we remained friends throughout the rest of the trip.

On the 10th day of the trip the *Coral Princess* glided up to the pier at Port Everglades, Ft. Lauderdale. The cruise was history and a bus was ready to take us back to Ft. Myers, our winter home. We will forever have our memories and photos of one of the most exciting trips we have ever taken.

Entering the Panama Canal.

LT and the Coral Princess in Jamaica.

CHAPTER THIRTY SEVEN

. . . the whole truth and nothing but the truth.

In November 2008, Granddaughter Jodi stated she had to interview a married couple and write up their experiences for a college class. (She also admitted she didn't know anyone who had been married for fifty years). After chatting a few minutes on the phone, we invited her to lunch at a nearby (for her) restaurant in Mt. Pleasant near the Central Michigan University campus where she was a sophomore.

Below, copied from our computer, is her paper in its entirety:

11/18/08

The Story of Lowell and Jane Thomas
Marriage Interview

How they met:

Lowell and Jane first met in the 4th grade. When the principal brought the new student in so she could meet everyone, Lowell knew he wouldn't like her. After all, Jane Lapworth had pigtails and a funny last name.

Growing up in a small town, everyone knows everyone else. That's exactly how it was for these two—it was hard to not spend time with one another when everyone has the same friends. They just always happened to attend the same social events.

In 7th grade, Lowell worked up the courage to ask Jane out for the first time. To Lowell's dismay, Jane turned him down. It would be 14 more years before he made another attempt at a date with Jane.

Recovering just fine, Lowell went on to date Jane's best friend during high school. It wasn't just him though—they both dated other people during high school.

After high school, Lowell was drafted into the Army and Jane left for college. They both went off to do their own things and live separate lives. Or so they thought . . .

Leading up to the Marriage:

On Lowell's second attempt at a date with Jane, their situations were a little different. Instead of two teenagers still in middle school, Jane was in her junior year of college and Lowell was recently out of the Army. This was the first time Jane started to look at him seriously.

However, after their first date, Jane returned home and told her mom, "Lowell is a nice guy, but we'll always just be friends."

Apparently, they were meant to be a lot more than Jane anticipated.

While the two were dating, they spent a lot of time traveling just to see one another. Jane was a student at Eastern Michigan University while Lowell was attending Western Michigan University.

They made it work though, and five months after he asked her out for the second time, they were engaged.

Lowell proposed to Jane on a freezing cold night in January while they were on a double date with another couple. He asked her to step out of the car for a minute, popped the question, and then told her to hurry up and answer because he was cold (what a romantic guy)!

That night, when Jane got back to her room, she broke down and cried, telling her roommate she had talked marriage with other boys before, but that this was really it. She couldn't have been more right.

Looking Back:

Of all the people in the world, these two were meant for each other. Lowell says he was just taking a chance because he didn't know all of the people in the world, and Jane says she knew he was the one because they had known each other for so long there were no surprises.

After fifty years of being together, they both agree that their main highlights were the birth of their children, outstanding careers in education and all of their travels around the world together.

Some things they say have made their marriage stronger is the fact that they've both had good, interesting jobs that they supported each other in, and that they do a lot of things together. Even when Lowell would have to go to conferences for work, Jane would accompany him.

One more thing that helped strengthen their bond was family time. They spent a lot of time together as a family; going camping, supporting their kids in their sports, and also just by valuing meal time as family time.

Another thing that Lowell and Jane agree on is that their marriage has had its struggles, too. They have a lot of good advice to offer on how to work through those tough times.

In their opinion, the biggest problem couples have today is a lack of communication. Because of their jobs, sometimes a husband and a wife aren't even together at dinnertime, and this causes a problem. According to them, it doesn't even matter what you talk about—you just have to talk about <u>something</u>.

Sometimes a relationship can even be considered work, but they think that if you just focus and stay on track, you can work through it—couples today just give up too easily. Jane will joke that they've had a lot to work through, but in the end it's easier to stay with

Lowell then to re-train someone else. There is some seriousness to her joking, however, because the 'work' to stay with Lowell really is worth it.

After fifty years together, you really get to know someone. Some more good advice they gave is to sometimes think of your spouse as a stranger. A big point they made was that the little things mean a lot. For example, even if they pour one another a cup of coffee, they still say thank you. People forget the niceties like that, and take for granted the little things. The way Jane puts it is that it may be taken for granted that she will have dinner on the table, but it's not taken for granted the fact that Lowell will help her to clean up afterwards.

Overall, they both agreed that it is very important not to go into a marriage thinking you are going to change someone. You have to accept that person for who they are and grow together.

Their own tough times:

After half a century of marriage, there is a lot to be learned from Lowell and Jane. Even though their marriage has had its good times, it's also had some bad. The two have attended marriage enrichment seminars and counseling even when they weren't having any problems, just to simply strengthen their bond.

The best advice they received, according to Jane, was from the counselor at their church. He used the analogy that marriage is like two pillars, and you have to have both of those pillars to hold the roof up.

Lowell also mentioned that marriage is not a 50/50 proposition, it's 100/100. Each person has to give 100% to make the marriage work. Both of those are extremely good ways to look at a relationship. It takes two people to make it work, and both of those people need to give 100%. Lowell also mentioned another very important key to marriage: the wife is never wrong; even when she is wrong, she is right. I think he's got the right idea!

Their parents' marriages:

The two said that in some ways their marriage was similar to their parents', and in other ways it is different. Time has changed and the cultures have changed. Lowell and Jane both said that their parents' had long lasting solid marriages.

One thing that Lowell mentioned was that when he was younger, he didn't realize his family was poor, but his dad was a carpenter and couldn't work in the winter, so they didn't have much money. He overheard his mother ask his father how they were going to pay the bills and his father replied that they would make it work. It was as simple as that—they just had faith in each other. You just have to have faith in each other to make it work. I think that is the simplest way to think of it.

Reflection:

I chose to interview my grandparents because they had just celebrated their 50th wedding anniversary, and that is an amazing accomplishment. I didn't want to write their story from a grandchild's point of view (I wasn't even around when this story took place!), which is why I chose to refer to them as Lowell and Jane instead of Grandpa and Grandma.

I really enjoyed this project, and learned a lot more than I expected to. I had no idea that my grandparents had known each other for so long before they started dating. Their story is a romantic one and I find it adorable that they met so long ago, and had no idea what was ahead of them. Also, I believe that their advice on how to make a relationship work is truly amazing advice. Everything they mentioned made perfect sense, and it is obviously effective.

Throughout the interview, they had a lot of funny answers to questions, some which I mentioned. For example, when I asked about tensions in the relationship, the only reply my grandpa had was . . . "Her mother". I think it is great that they still joke around like that, and they still have fun with each other. It is just one more of those 'little things' that really help.

As an ending to the interview, Jane shared with me that it is the greatest compliment to have her granddaughter ask for help on a

Project like this because it is their greatest wish that all of their grandchildren find happiness. They've certainly provided all of us grandchildren with the best role models.

I hope that one day I find what they've found in each other—true love and happiness.

Good grief! What insight and wisdom comes from a 19-year-old college student. Little did Jane and I realize, at the time, just how much Jodi had absorbed over our conversation at lunch.

After she had e-mailed us a copy, I wrote back and said, "I want your prof's name, address and social security number. If he doesn't give you an "A" on the paper, I'll make his life a living hell." She received the "A." That took a lot of pressure off me too.

CHAPTER THIRTY EIGHT

Some people get it right!

2009 held a couple surprises. Brother Bruce and our son Dave had gone to the famous Indy 500 race in Indianapolis the year before. They enjoyed it so much they asked me to go along this year. Anyone who knows me knows I don't give a hoot about cars, especially horrendously noisy ones traveling over 200 mph, crashing into walls and into each other. In fact, if my own car stops I might as well open the trunk as open the hood. I get the same results. But I don't care. That's what mechanics are for.

(Back in the early '60's I decided I could save money by changing my own oil. The first time I tried it, I drained the oil out of the transmission instead of the crank case (I think those are the terms). I didn't save any money. But that's another story. Now back to this one).

So I surprised everyone, including myself, by accepting the offer to attend the Indy. And surprisingly, I had a marvelous time. Not at the race, but watching and talking with people from all over the country who thought the Indy 500 was God's greatest gift to humanity.

But more than anything, I enjoyed being in the company of Bruce and Dave. What party animals! It was tough for this "old man" to keep up. But well worth the effort.

We were gone for three nights; one night at Bruce's who lived within driving distance (from Three Rivers, MI), one night in Kokomo, IN, about an hour from Indianapolis with much cheaper motels, then another night in Kokomo, with a three-hour drive back to Bruce's the following day.

Now for the second surprise. One night while we were away, Jane had a mysterious caller at the house. She was certain someone was trying to get in the front door. It was after dark; she was alarmed and frightened. Quietly calling 911, she announced her situation. Within minutes a State

Police car was in our driveway. One officer knocked on the door while the other walked around the house with a flashlight.

It had been raining and the officer's footprints, with the porch light gleaming off them, showed on the wooden porch leading to the front door. There were other prints there as well. The officer noticed those of a small animal, probably a raccoon, leading to the woodpile next to the door. Evidently, the animal, climbing the pile caused the wood to slide, creating the noise Jane had heard.

Not mildly embarrassed (but <u>highly</u> embarrassed), she apologized for calling the police. But the highly trained officers made her feel at ease and were appreciative of her call. (It must have been a routinely dull evening for them).

But we three went again to the races again in 2010. This time there were five of us; Dave, Bruce, grandson Kevin, nephew Jim Carr and myself. It was the hottest day on record at the Indy; a sweltering, humid 90 degrees in the stands and 130 degrees on the track. I survived only by leaving the stands, sitting in the shade of the stands, placing a towel on my head and pouring cold water from a bottle on the towel. I was able to listen to the cars as they thundered around the track. Yeah, like that's really fun!! Dave and Bruce would join me periodically, but Kevin and Jim sweat it out in the stands for the entire race.

I told the guys this was my last Indy. Undaunted, Bruce suggested that I come along the following year and stay in the motel in Kokomo on race day. I could bring my laptop computer and a book and still enjoy the company and partying in the evenings, both at Bruce's and at the motel. Since I am both a writer and a reader, I agreed that that is what I would do. And I am doing just that in the motel room in 2011 in Kokomo. As the race goes on, I am editing *So Far . . . So Good . . . So There!*

That night in the motel room, however, I decided that this would, indeed, be my last Indy. I can read and write at home.

What made the decision final, however, was that after the others had been at the race for three hours, they returned to the room only to turn on the TV and watch another three hours of the race, from beginning to end. During that time we played cards. Fifteen minutes before the race ended I picked up the remote and muted the TV, saying, "Guys, I'm sorry. I know you love this sport but I just can't handle that constant noise (the race cars thundering around the track at over 200 mph)."

Our game was nearly over, and when it ended the others went into an adjoining room to watch the finale.

I felt terrible and apologized to Dave and Bruce for my attitude and prepared for bed. As these words go on paper I'm not entirely certain I was forgiven.

But on the 2010 trip, the most enjoyable event occurred in the motel dining room the day following the race. I wrote it up and submitted it to the *Midland Daily News* for publication as a "Letter to the Editor." It was titled, *Some People Get It Right,* and it went like this:

> *On Memorial Day Weekend my son and I, a grandson, a brother and a nephew attended the Indy 500 in Indianapolis. Despite the hoopla leading up to the beginning of the race; the American flag (the size of a football field) being unfurled on the infield while Florence Henderson sang the Star Spangled Banner and four Air Force jets in formation thundered overhead, and the race itself . . . the weekend held an even greater thrill for me.*
>
> *At breakfast in the dining area of our motel the following morning, three youngsters of Asian descent, probably in age from six to ten, were eating there as well. My son, trying to be friendly, used his total vocabulary of five words in Japanese, and getting no response from them, asked in English, "Are you Japanese? Chinese?" Without missing a beat the eldest of the three answered with, "We are American."*
>
> *God bless them and God bless America!*

A surgery I had mentioned in my book, *So Far . . . So Good . . . The Other Lowell Thomas Story,* told of my having surgery for an enlarged prostate. I mentioned it only because my father had had the same surgery and that if it can be inherited, my son and grandson and their male offspring should be alerted.

What I didn't mention, however, was that prior to my surgery my PSA rating stood at 4.5, a bit on the high side. A month afterward it was 0.07. What I didn't mention also was that each time I would e-mail brother, Bruce, I would sign off with 0.07 and he knew why. He once mentioned that I was a "007," the name of a famous movie about a romantic/detective type guy who, through many misadventures, always solved the case and ended up with the most beautiful woman in the movie.

I say all this only to mention that I'm undoubtedly the only author in history who ever signed his name using his PSA status. (Now that's worth knowing, isn't it? And aren't you glad you have read this story this far?).

CHAPTER THIRTY NINE

As one ages, we tend to use more four letter words, i.e.,
What? When?

As one ages, many things can happen to the body. For me, it enlarged during 2009. Not just around the middle, but I developed a "ledge" in my throat. Nothing to necessarily be alarmed about, but if food doesn't gracefully slip off the ledge, it results in severe coughing. One solution is to wash it down with the nearest available liquid, another is to hack it up and spit it out. The former is preferable, but doesn't always work. It can also be embarrassing in a restaurant or other public place. Sometimes even saliva can set off the coughing.

One thing the surgeon suggested was to eat slower. I wanted to inform him that if I ate slower at breakfast, it would be time for lunch, but I didn't. Several years before I had to have two molars extracted, one on each side of my mouth. I didn't realize until then how important those molars were. When others in my dining group would be finished eating, I would still have a fourth-to-half of my meal left. Sometimes it was embarrassing when we had friends in for dinner because they were anxious to go to the next step . . . dessert and/or playing cards, which we all loved.

I had had all the tests available, provided by a local ear, nose and throat (ENT) specialist who referred me to another specialist at the University of Michigan in Ann Arbor.

The bottom line is explained in the following e-mail message I sent to family and friends who were concerned. It went like this:

Date: September 10, 2009

Subject: I'm a One!

    Yesterday, now that was a different day; full of new experiences, a disappointment and continuing education. On Tuesday (Sept. 8) we received a call from the U. of M. Hospital that my surgery time would be 10:30 a.m.

    That meant we would leave the house at 5:45 a.m. so we could arrive at the hospital two hours prior to surgery (their request). We don't like driving that time of day/night in deer country, but didn't spot any until we were coming back, less than two miles from home, and in broad daylight.

    Anyway, we walked up to the receptionist's desk at exactly 8:29 a. m. (that included a MacDonald's break near Flint to get Jane some breakfast. I wasn't allowed any food after midnight and no liquids after 6:30 a.m.). We were so grateful to be there early so we could wait another three hours to be called into pre-op. Little wonder . . . the waiting room was the size of a small gymnasium . . . only not as sweaty even as it began to fill up.

    About 9:30, daughter, Brenda, showed up even though we told her it wouldn't be necessary. We were pleased she did. By that time Jane and I were tired of talking to each other and smiling at strangers. Stress is not always a good thing.

    At 11:30 it was finally our turn in the pre-op room . . . my turn actually, since I was the only one being pre-opted. But visitors were allowed. It would have been pretty boring if they weren't as that took another hour to hook up some machinery, tubes and . . . waiting.

    One of the anesthesiologists (thank God for spell-check), a 40ish, somewhat pretty lady with a sense of humor, was working on a computer next to my bed, asking questions which she punched in and turning to talk with me on the bed and to Jane and Brenda on the other side. As she would turn, she would casually place one hand on my thigh (oh stop it, I had a hospital gown on and a blanket over me!). At one point, she, without thinking . . . I think . . . turned to talk and placed a hand on the "general." They used to be "privates" but as one matures, they get promoted and I finally got a general.

I told Jane later that if I hadn't been getting groggy from the I-V, I'm sure something would have happened to embarrass everyone in the room.

But all the people at the hospital were just more than helpful, cordial and congenial. That included the receptionists on up through the surgeon. In fact, one of the receptionists, upon request, copied a delicious-looking pie recipe for Jane, from a magazine.

Now for the disappointing part . . . in post-op the surgeon explained that the "ledge" in my throat, which was trapping food going south, was too far down the esophagus to reach with the equipment that was made for the purpose. So all he left me with was a temporary sore throat from the probing, and a slightly chipped front tooth (which we had, prior to surgery, been informed could happen). So before we left the hospital we were ushered (me in a wheel chair because I was still a bit groggy) to the dental section where a very friendly dentist ground the chip flat with the rest of the tooth. He made some remark about the "other" Lowell Thomas, so that says something for his age.

But back to the surgeon . . . he gave us two options to think about:

1) He could still take care of the "ledge" through an open incision. Problems: There is a greater chance of infection, there is a slight chance of injuring the voice box and it would leave a four-inch scar on my throat. Someone from the hospital will call within a week to reschedule surgery to see if I want to go that way.

2) Live with it. I think I'll opt for the latter. Shucks, I probably won't have more than another 40 years or so to put up with it anyway.

He also said that my situation happens to about one in ten people. So there . . . I'm a one! Nine other people can't say that.

Since we thought I would be staying overnight at the hospital, Jane had made arrangements to stay at (a shuttle-bus ride away) the nearest Holiday Inn. Brenda took charge and called the motel to cancel her reservation. Just as well too. The e-mail confirmation we received a week ago had her listed as "James Thomas." We might not have had a room.

They must have pumped me full of fluids through the I-V during surgery (plus I sipped ice water all the way home to cool my throat and to make the swelling recede). Jane had to drive the 130 miles home, but had to stop four times for me to the use restrooms at MacDonald's or gas stations. Had to go twice more within an hour of arriving home as well. This might be more information than you need/want to know.

I didn't talk much on the way home because of the soreness in the throat, and slept some of the way, but when I did speak Jane said I sounded "sexy." I'm betting Medicare and Blue Cross/Blue Shield will be turned on too.

As I write this, the swelling in my throat and the soreness has diminished immensely. My next sip of liquid will be a Scotch!

Thanks to all for your e-mails, cards, calls and concerns. If I didn't have friends and family, I would have nobody. God bless you all!

Lowell

*　*　*

If I learned anything in my thirty four years in education, it was that human beings are not machines. Machines can be perfected, humans cannot. One year while working for the Midland Public Schools, an elementary principal wrote a grant to a local foundation for $5,000. It was to replace aging playground equipment for his school. The superintendent, upon learning of the awarding of the grant, told the principal it could not be accepted because no other elementary school was getting an award.

Sure, the principal should have checked with the superintendent first (and saved himself a lot of work), but instead of crediting the principal with his innovative spirit and setting an example of what could be done if one applied himself, the superintendent simply denied the money.

That's only one example of working for an ultra-conservative boss I witnessed over the twenty-three years I was with the Midland Public Schools. Other innovative ideas which were shot down, I personally experienced over the years. In spite of that, being the director of adult and continuing education for twenty years was the best and most inspiring job I had in my lifetime. It taught me much about people and how to get them to work for and with you.

In my frustration, and those of others, I came up with something that was put to calligraphy on colored poster board and framed by a dear friend, Denise Spencer, with whom I had worked for many years. At the time, Denise was director of the Midland Foundation and had served on my adult education advisory council. It read:

If you follow the book by the letter, the only mistake you can make is following the book by the letter.

The proclamation hung in my adult education office, as a reminder, through the 1970's, and until I retired from the Midland Public Schools in 1987. After I retired, I gave the framed plaque to son, David so he could remember it as well. He too worked with facets of the human population as the 4-H Youth Director for Midland County and the Michigan State University Extension Office.

CHAPTER FORTY

Life isn't tied with a bow,
but it's still a gift.

As 2010 came to a close, Jane and I had been blessed with events we hadn't even dreamed about during over fifty years of marriage. On May 22 (the day before my 74th birthday), granddaughter Ashley Thomas became the beautiful bride of Benjamin (Ben) Trumpeter. She had just completed her requirements for a R.N. at Hope College in Holland, Michigan. Ben continues his education as a firefighter and EMS attendant as this is being written. They live in Kalamazoo where Ben is also employed in his field and Ashley works at Spectrum Butterworth Hospital in Grand Rapids. Although living in Clare, the wedding took place on a beautiful hill overlooking a plush valley in Traverse City, Michigan.

The other blessed event came on October 23 (two days after Jane's 74th birthday). It was a gorgeous autumn day in Clare, Michigan when granddaughter Stacy Thomas took Benjamin (Ben) Ashworth as her life mate. Stacy was as gorgeous as was the day. How ironic that these two beautiful sisters both married a man named Benjamin. Stacy's Ben was originally from California. Also ironic is that both girls met their betrothed at the same Bible camp on Gull Lake, near Battle Creek, and worked there together for a number of years in the summers. Stacy and her Ben moved to Bensonville (also ironic), Illinois, near Chicago, where Ben is a Financial Aid Counselor for Wheaton College, his Alma Mater.

CHAPTER FORTY ONE

We don't always appreciate what we have
until we don't have it anymore.

We may sometimes think we have problems, but we were reminded that there are others who suffer much worse. A catastrophe occurred on March 11, 2011, that nearly brought the entire planet to its knees . . . an earthquake, rated to be a "9" on a ten point scale, a tsunami with waves over thirty feet high behind a tidal wave traveling at 500 miles an hour rattled nearly the whole island of Honshu, Japan. The ensuing waves knocked out an atomic generator plant in northeastern Japan, and is causing radiation fear yet as this being written (mid-April 2011).

Our dear friends, Michiko and Yoshi Takahashi live less than 150 miles from that plant in the Prefecture of Fukushima. The two of them have been to our home on Wixom Lake. Michiko visited us in our winter home in Ft. Myers, FL as recently as April of 2011. And we had visited them in their home in 2001.

We immediately exchanged e-mails and found that while they were safe, the quake was felt by them, and Yoshi who is a carpenter, had to replace their earthquake-damaged wooden steps leading to their front door.

Later in March we received the following e-mail from Michiko:

March 31, 2011

Hello Jane and Lowell,

    We are okay nothing change. Luckily we can get gasoline without standing a long line. Last week, I stood in a line for 4 hours to get 12 liters gasoline. Did you believe it? I was really lucky to get it for only 4 hours.Many people stood in a line a night to get only 12 liters. But We can get some gasoline this week!!!! I am happy!! Also we can buy some kerosene this week! We were so cold we could not buy kerosene last week. We have electricity but we hesitate to use air conditioner because the radiation problem. Some people in Shirakawa use air conditioners and I think it is okay now (We do not have children and we are not young people. Babies and little children have to care about drinking water, vegetables and using many things. We are not babies,ha.ha)

You went to Iwaki with us to have picnic. Iwaki takes 50 kilometers south from the nuclear plants. It is not safer than here Shirakawa but my friend Mikiko and her family you met still live there. I have another friend who was born in this town lives in Iwaki as a junior high teacher. She does not come back to Shirakawa. Many people out of 30kilometers away from the plants still do not move. Because we think if we move another place to evacuate,we could not live comfortably. If we move another place, we should stay a gym and sleep on a cold floor with a thin blanket. They can eat a lot but it is cold and do not use a clean bath and so on. I do not think it is good. We can sleep a warm Futon and can eat, use a bath, of course my friends in Iwaki think same thing.

If the plants had a big problem, we got same destiny as if we live in Tokyo or that area. Japan is a small island, it is 150-200kilometers from Fukushima to Tokyo (I think), we could not run anywhere. So I believe our country and our destiny. Yoshi and I do not care about the plants and try to keep normal life. So please do not worry about us. I bought some Andes mint chocolate yesterday and remember you both. It was yummy chocolate!!!

My mom and Yoshi's parents stay their homes and live usual:-) Yoshi fixes some houses in Shirakawa. Our house is okay all windows, walls and a roof did not broke though many tableware were broken but some in Shirakawa broke many things such as roofs, walls and important parts in their houses. Yoshi is fixing a house for his friend's parent's house.

We do not need anything but prayers. Thank you, thank you again. I can not believe I was in Florida last spring. Please tell your friends there, Michiko is eating American chocolate with smile. Yum, yum.

Love and hugs,xoxoxoxoxo
Michiko, Yoshi and Hime (Hime is their dog).

Being optimists seems to be a part of the Japanese culture, and the Takahashi's carry that well.

Another Japanese couple whom we befriended is Nobu and Shimaku Tomono. Through the local 4-H program we stayed at their home a week in 2001 and they have since been to our home on Wixom Lake. They live on the Chiba Peninsula, just south of Tokyo, where the earthquake was also felt.

When we e-mailed them following the disaster, we heard nothing for many days. Finally, we received the message below:

Tuesday, March 15, 2011 4:41 PM

Lowell and Jane,

So sorry, our main phone (light) and thus URL was down up to afternoon yesterday 15th.

Yes, we are all safe, but traffic is very wrong. On 11th I was at Makurari Messe where I was making year-end tax arrangement application. On way back to home, we were obliged to walk two hours. On Monday 14th, I attended the company I belong. Usually it is 1-hour traffic, which took over 2-hours.

But still we have no trouble at all on life line, thanks to God.

We do appreciate your sympathy.

Sincerely yours,
Shimako and Nobu

Whenever we think we have problems we think of Michiko, Yoshi, Nobu and Shimako.

Michiko and Jane at the Ft. Myers Airport

CHAPTER FORTY TWO

And as I stand now in the twilight of life and retrospect the past,
I feel that I surely have been led by a kind Providence all my days
in paths I have not known. I have much for which to be thankful.
                                                —Thomas Hawkins

I don't know the author of the above paragraph, but it certainly sums up the thoughts on my life. I truly have much for which to be thankful. And it is certainly summed up earlier in this memoir in the essay titled, *Happy Anniversary, Sweetheart.* It was written on our 35th anniversary and was written for my radio broadcast over WGDN in Gladwin. It is as true today as it was the day I wrote it and can be found on earlier pages.

Both Jane and I have had illnesses and surgeries throughout our 50+ years together. But we have stayed the course. Jane has suffered with breast cancer and has suffered the traumas of chemotherapy and radiation. She has had all her toe joints removed due to arthritis and both knee joints replaced.

Her most lasting illness, however, if it can be called that, is her essential involuntary head tremor. She inherited it through her genes from her mother, Gladys Lapworth.

Jane doesn't know when her head is in a tremor stage, but if I mention it to her she can stop it by merely changing the angle of her head ever so slightly. Whenever we are in public and her head unknowingly begins to bob, we have had a code. I will get her attention and rub the side of my nose. She then can stop the tremor, even though temporarily.

What she *didn't* inherit from her mother, is her voice tremor. Making light of it, she says she might someday be as famous as Kathryn Hepburn, a movie star from our youth who was also afflicted with such. (Nah, that won't happen).

Sometimes while speaking, her voice will tremor and I will have to ask her to repeat it. Making it worse is the fact that over recent years I have been having a slight hearing loss. So when her voice cracks, she thinks it is my hearing and I think it is her voice cracking. Neither of us has ever won that argument.

Fortunately, there has been a temporary treatment for Jane's voice; a glass of wine. Her doctor confirmed that, but unfortunately, couldn't give her a prescription for it. One day, about 5:30 p.m., Jane was talking on the telephone with our friend, Sandie Butler. At one point, Sandie said, "You're having a glass of wine, aren't you?" Jane's voice had been smooth throughout the conversation.

The only reason I even mention this affliction of Jane's is because it may someday show up in the genes of some of our descendants. We are thankful that a tremor is not life threatening. We have been blessed with an understanding family and friends.

CHAPTER FORTY THREE

It's not what you gather, but what you scatter
that tells what kind of life you have lived.

Life has been good to Jane and me, and we have been good for each other. In several undergraduate business classes on the way to a degree, the professor would say something like, "Look ahead and decide where you want to be five years or ten years from now." Yeah, right. Most of the time Jane and I didn't know where we would be the following week, and it didn't matter. We only knew we loved each other and took each day at a time and made plans as we went along. Most of the time it worked.

And believe it or not, it all worked out just fine. We have owned a nice home on a quiet, shady street in Midland, Michigan (for nearly thirty years), where Brenda and David could walk to every public school they attended and I could walk to work for many years. We also owned two cottages (not at the same time) on Wixom Lake; one in Midland County and one in Gladwin County, plus built a beautiful permanent home on that lake in 1992 where we share fantastic sunsets.

We have both had great careers in education and have produced two great kids who have produced five beautiful grand kids. Plus, we have had the resources to travel to several parts of the world; from Hawaii to Alaska, to New Zealand, to Japan, to the Fiji Islands in the Pacific as well as several countries in Europe, the Mediterranean, the Caribbean, Mexico, Canada and most of the lower forty-eight States.

Since 2001 we have owned a double-wide mobile home in Ft. Myers, Florida, where we spend up to five months each winter, and have made friends with many wonderful people from around the United States with whom we often get together, even in the summers; either at their homes or at ours on the lake. Fortunately, our winter home is in one of the finest, cleanest and best run mobile home parks in all of Florida. There are only

151 units there (many parks in our area have several hundred units) and it is like living in a community where everyone knows nearly everyone else. The only downside is that it is sometimes in a hurricane lane during the summer and early fall months. In 2004 Hurricane Charley caused us $16,000 in damages to our winter home. Thanks to insurance, our payout was only $2,000.

In addition, we have had the privilege of having Brother Bruce and wife, Jeanette, rent close to us in our park for a month or so for a few winters and we all enjoyed the beaches, restaurants and movie theaters.

Our winter home in Ft. Myers.

Spring colors in Ft. Myers.

Sunset from our deck on Wixom Lake. So sad it is not in color.

CHAPTER FORTY FOUR

You realize you are never going to be good at anything . . .
unless you care.

There has been a standing joke in our family, and that joke has been me. I feel compelled to enter it in this memoir because it has been so much a part of my life.

My father was gifted when it came to working with his hands. He was a brilliant carpenter and could build and fix most anything. Early in his life, he was known as an industrial arts teacher. In today's educational jargon, it is simply a woodshop teacher (I think).

Unfortunately, Dad didn't have the patience to teach me much of that and I probably had little patience for learning it anyway. It was simply easier for him to do it all himself. I certainly had no gift for it and really, I didn't care.

If something needed fixing around our house, Jane could normally do it. If something mechanical needed to be repaired, Jane could do it or we would call on a friend or family who has the knowledge and skills. And sometimes we would even hire it done by a professional.

Whenever friends are in a conversation about fixing something, I will often say, "Yeah, I would have done it that way too." Most of the time I don't even know what they are talking about, they know that, and they get a good laugh . . . at me. I do love to see people laugh.

Fortunately, I have possessed attributes that others do not have that has made me successful in other ways.

* * *

Someone once said that, "Good judgment comes from experience. Unfortunately, experience comes from bad judgment." In my seventy-five years I have learned how true that is; sometimes from my own bad judgment, and sometimes from the experiences and bad judgment of those close to me.

An anonymous writer pretty much hit the nail on the head by putting to paper the following, all of which I truly believe, and which I wish I had come up with first. I doctored a few of the below myself just to make them more personal and which better fit my own philosophies.

I'VE LEARNED THAT . . .

When you're in love, it shows.

Just one person saying to me, "You've made my day!" makes my day.

Being kind is more important than being right.

I can always pray for someone when I don't have the strength or wisdom to help him/her in some other way.

No matter how serious your life requires you to be, everyone needs a friend to act goofy with.

Sometimes all a person needs is a hand to hold and a heart to understand.

Love, not time, heals all wounds.

The easiest way for me to succeed as a person is to surround myself with people smarter than I am.

No one is perfect until you fall in love with them.

I wish I could have told my Mom that I loved her one more time before she passed away.

One should keep his words both soft and tender because tomorrow he may have to eat them.

A smile is an inexpensive way to improve your looks.

When your newly born grandchild holds your little finger in his little fist, you're hooked for life.

Everyone wants to live on top of the mountain, but all the happiness and growth occurs while you're climbing it.

Friends, where would we be without them?

And my own personal favorite, which I purchased for Jane on one of our many trips and still sets, in a small frame, on a lamp stand near our front window where we often read, and says:

> *Tough times don't last . . . . tough people do.*

I gave it to her when she was going through chemotherapy following her breast surgery for cancer in 2002.

EPILOGUE

Life is too short to wake up with regrets. So love the people who treat you right. Forget about those who don't. Believe everything happens for a reason. If you get a chance, take it. If it changes your life, let it. Nobody said life would be easy, they just promised it would most likely be worth it.

To put it another way, the cartoon character, Maxine once said, "Be who you are and say what you feel because those that matter don't mind and those that mind don't matter."

*   *   *

Someone also said, "If you are a writer, write something you know something about." I have done that by writing this book. I have learned much about who I am and who I have been. My hope is that my descendants, by reading this, will know who I am and know from which they came.